MW01121982

160201

Canada On Stage

Scenes and Monologues

…a survey of Canadian theatre…

Canada
On Stage

Scenes and Monologues

…a survey of Canadian theatre…

Edited by Iris Turcott and Keith Turnbull

Playwrights Canada Press
Toronto • Canada

Canada On Stage: Scenes and Monologues © 2006 Iris Turcott, Keith Turnbull
The moral rights of the authors are asserted.

Playwrights Canada Press
215 Spadina Avenue, Suite 230, Toronto, Ontario CANADA M5T 2C7
416-703-0013 fax 416-408-3402
orders@playwrightscanada.com • www.playwrightscanada.com

This book would be twice its cover price were it not for the support of Canadian taxpayers through the Government of Canada Book Publishing Industry Development Programme, Canada Council for the Arts, Ontario Arts Council and the Ontario Media Development Corporation.

Front cover painting: Bill Bragg "Performers", Oil on Canvas, 69 by 48 inches.
Original artwork can be viewed at www.theartark.com/bragg
A print of "Performers" is also available through the Art Ark Gallery.
Production Editing/Cover Design: JLArt

Library and Archives Canada Cataloguing in Publication

Canada on stage : scenes and monologues / edited by Iris Turcott and Keith Turnbull.

Includes index.
ISBN 978-0-88754-888-8

1. Canadian drama (English)--20th century. 2. Monologues, Canadian (English). I. Turnbull, Keith II. Turcott, Iris

PS8307.C34 2006   C812'.5408   C2006-902361-1

First edition: May 2006. Second printing: June 2008.
Printed and bound by Canadian Printco at Scarborough, Canada.

All works in this book, *Canada On Stage: Scenes and Monologues*, are copyrighted in the playwright's name. Where not noted on this page, permission to copy or use the work in any way, may be made through Playwrights Canada Press (see copyright page for contact information). Where noted below, permission made be made directly to the publisher (see page 229 for contact information).

Acknowledgements

Talonbooks

The Shape of a Girl, Joan MacLeod
Burning Vision, Marie Clements
Earshot, Morris Panych
Fronteras Americanas,
   Guillermo Verdecchia
The Vic, Leanna Brodie
Little Sister, Joan MacLeod
Consecrated Ground, George Boyd
Unity (1918), Kevin Kerr
The Ventriloquist, Larry Tremblay
Featuring Loretta, George F. Walker

Signature Editions

Walking on Water, Dave Carley

Brooklyn Publishers, LLC

Orders, Sandra Dempsey

Leméac Éditeur

Alphonse, Wajdi Mouawad

Scirocco Drama

The Orphan Muses,
   Michel Marc Bouchard
Grace, Michael Lewis MacLennan
fareWel, Ian Ross
cherry docs, David Gow
Liar, Brian Drader
Therac 25, Adam Pettle

Carol Shields Literary Trust

Unless, Sara Cassidy and Carol Shields

McArthur & Company

The Harps of God, Kent Stetson

Breton Books

Hockey Mom, Hockey Dad,
   Michael Melski

Table of Contents

About the Editors

Iris Turcott has been the company dramaturge at the Canadian Stage Company for the past 14 years. Prior to CanStage, she was a freelance dramaturge, director and actor. She was also co-founder and co-Artistic Director of Playbill Theatre. Iris has worked with playwrights from coast to coast including Adam Pettle, Joan MacLeod, Michel Marc Bouchard, Brad Fraser, Judith Thompson, Sunil Kuruvilla and Tomson Highway. She has been involved in a number of international co-commissions including the Royal Exchange in Manchester, the Melbourne Festival and the Abbey Theatre. She is also the dramaturge for Ronnie Burkett's internationally acclaimed Theatre of Marionettes. Iris is active in Arts Education and is involved in a number of aspects of publishing. She is currently serving on the Board of Directors for the LMDA (Literary Managers and Dramaturgs of the Americas).

Keith Turnbull is a director, dramaturge and producer committed to contemporary and new work in theatre and opera. He was artistic director of the Manitoba Theatre Centre; of Second Stage, Neptune Theatre; and founding artistic director of the NDWT Co. with which he started a First Nations theatre company from which emerged many of Canada's most noted native performers and writers. He is the past Artistic Director/ Executive Producer of Banff Theatre Arts. He has taught extensively throughout Canada.

He has directed more than ninety plays in theatres across Canada and opera/ music theatre in Canada, Wales, Sweden, and USA. He is directing *A Chair in love*, a new comic opera by John Metcalf and Larry Tremblay this June in Montreal.

Scenes

1 female
1 male

Tempting Providence

by Robert Chafe

*Premiered at Gros Morne Theatre Festival, Newfoundland,
produced by Theatre Newfoundland Labrador, 2002*

Script available from Playwrights Canada Press

•

Myra, a young British nurse, is being courted by a native
Newfoundlander, Angus. The year is 1921.

•

MYRA   My lord, it is hot in there.

ANGUS   Is that why we are out here?

MYRA   You people, it's amazing. This perfectly nice house, with
a perfectly nice parlour, couches, chairs, and you all insist upon
squeezing into a kitchen the size of a closet.

ANGUS   It's a proper dance my dear. Can't stray from the kitchen.

MYRA   Really.

ANGUS   You complaining?

MYRA   What?

ANGUS   You weren't having fun?

MYRA   I simply said it was hot.

ANGUS   Think I didn't notice the circle you were spinning around that
room with Alex? Cut a path right into the floorboards no doubt. I told
Mother not to invite you, you would only do damage.

MYRA   I didn't say I wasn't enjoying myself Mr. Bennett.

ANGUS   You're just hot.

MYRA   Warm. Yes. Too warm.

ANGUS   Now see that sounds like the words of a woman who is not planning on walking back into that kitchen for one more dance.

MYRA   I honestly don't think I'm up for it.

ANGUS   You are going home after having the last dance with Alex. That's not a slap in the face is it.

MYRA   Your brother was very insistent.

ANGUS   Runs in the family. Just like our dancing. Give me half the chance, I'll prove it.

MYRA   Your insistence?

ANGUS   You're not going home yet.

MYRA   Excuse me?

ANGUS   Unless you want half the town thinking you're only after younger men.

MYRA   Inappropriate, Mr. Bennett.

ANGUS   I agree. Doesn't become you.

MYRA   Stop it. What do I have to say? What would you have me do?

ANGUS   Take five minutes. Long enough to catch your breath.

Another silent standoff. She holds his gaze, and then looks up at the sky.

MYRA   Lovely night. You have a lot of them here.

ANGUS   Yes. I keep forgetting that our beloved nurse has only been with us since the spring. She has not has the pure pleasure of a Newfoundland winter.

MYRA   You all have this big talk about winter. Like it's a terror. You're not frightening me. I don't scare off that easily.

ANGUS   No?

MYRA   I, my dear man, have battled and braved worse foes than your much vilified Newfoundland winter.

ANGUS   So you think.

MYRA   You are so smug, Mr. Bennett. How can you be sure that I do not have a fondness for a little snow and wind?

He laughs.

How can you be sure Mr. Bennett that your lengthy winter is not one of the reasons I chose to come to Newfoundland in the first place?

ANGUS   Was it?

MYRA   As a matter of fact, yes.

ANGUS   Our winters and our kitchen parties.

A small pause.

What were your reasons?

MYRA   What?

ANGUS   Why did you come here?

A small pause.

MYRA   No great secret, I wanted to help. I wanted to help people.

ANGUS   Newfoundlanders.

MYRA   Newfoundlanders. Anybody.

ANGUS   Could of helped anybody in England. Didn't need to come all the way over here to do that.

MYRA   It was a question of need. There was a great and saddening need here. I read a story about a family in Saskatchewan. I originally applied to go there. And was told I was needed more here.

ANGUS   One story about one family and you packed up your life?

MYRA   A young mother, her first child. She and her husband lived quite a distance out. Quite a few days travel to anybody else. He left to get help. Left as soon as they thought the baby might be on its way. Weather set in. Help was too far away. Hours turn into days. Story has a sad ending.

ANGUS   And that was that? Duty calls?

MYRA   Stories about mothers and babies deserve only the happiest of endings.

A small pause. He smiles at her.

ANGUS   They are all afraid of you, you know. Terrified. Gotta do what the Nurse says or else.

She looks at the sky silently.

MYRA   It's necessary sometimes, to make myself clear, and listened to.

ANGUS   Oh you don't have to tell me. It's just… I think they see this one side of you. They see this Nurse. A very good Nurse, well respected, don't get me wrong. But they just see that side. And that's a shame. Because… I get the feeling that Nurse Grimsley has a depth that would make the very Atlantic blush with shame.

She remains staring at the sky.

MYRA   Mr. Bennett—

ANGUS   Your five minutes are up.

She looks at him.

Do you have your breath?

A warm pause.

MYRA   I believe so.

ANGUS   Yes?

MYRA   Take me back to your hot and crowded kitchen. If you must.

ANGUS laughs.

ANGUS   If I must?

MYRA   If you must, take me to your kitchen sir. Dance me until my legs themselves plead for clemency.

The Unforgetting

by Alan Dilworth

Premiered at the SummerWorks Festival, Toronto, 2004

Script available from the Playwrights Guild of Canada

•

"Did my father do this?"

Percy and Devon find a stranger's book containing sketches
showing Percy's father killing a man and laying him in the ground.
Percy burns the book, then the phone rings with the news.

•

DEVON   There has been an accident. The man is dead.

Beat.

We have to go and find out if there is a body buried behind the mill.

PERCY   What are you talking about?

DEVON   Percy, there was a picture of your father laying a man in the
ground.

PERCY   You want to dig a hole to see if my father killed a man?

DEVON   We only have a few hours of daylight left.

PERCY   You want to— Devon turns and walks out the door.

DEVON enters with two shovels in hand.

DEVON   One for you and one for me.

PERCY   You think I'm going to dig?

DEVON crosses to upstage curtains.

DEVON   Across the bridge. We know where the sketches say it happened.

PERCY crosses to upstage curtains.

PERCY   Around the bend. Clouds moving in.

DEVON   And behind the mill. Here we are.

PERCY   Walker's Point.

BOTH   Miller's Rock.

PERCY   Devon standing spade in hand.

DEVON   It looks like rain. I guess we should get started.

PERCY   Not a bird chirps, not a leaf flutters.

DEVON   Shall we say a quick prayer?

PERCY   Yes.

They pray.

PERCY   Devon's spade rises up and hits the earth.

DEVON   The grass is thick, you have to push hard.

PERCY   The first clump of soil is dropped by the side.

DEVON   This could take some time.

PERCY   Spade after spade we dig into the ground. We work and we work until we're up to our knees.

DEVON   How are your hands?

PERCY   Fine. Yours?

DEVON   Fine.

PERCY   And we dig and we dig, until we're up to his waist.

DEVON   So far, so good. According to those pictures it shouldn't be much deeper than this.

PERCY   We should have found him by now.

DEVON   Why don't you take a rest. And I dig and I dig.

PERCY   And I take a rest.

DEVON   Phew. I don't know. I think that's it.

PERCY   And he wipes his brow.

DEVON   So much for those pictures.

PERCY   Amen.

DEVON   Well—

PERCY   And he stands his spade straight up in—

DEVON   Crunch.

PERCY   Devon? What is it?

DEVON   Go get me a sheet from the house.

PERCY   What is it?

DEVON   Go get me a sheet.

PERCY   This can't be true.

DEVON   Percy, go!

> *PERCY exits.*

Bone after bone uncovered in dirt.

> *PERCY enters.*

PERCY   In through the front door and up the stairs. Cupboard door opens... I move my father's prayer box off to the side. Pillowcase, pillowcase, old cotton sheet.... Across the bridge, around the bend, behind the mill.... There must be some—

> *DEVON grabs the sheet from PERCY.*

DEVON   A perfect skeleton lies sleeping in the ground. We'll wrap them up and move them till we decide what to do.... Here take this...

PERCY   Did my father do this?

> *DEVON turns to leave, a bundle of bones in his hand.*

PERCY   Where are we taking them?

DEVON   The basement.

PERCY   Our basement?

DEVON   Beneath the stairs where we keep the wood.

PERCY   We can't.

DEVON   Just until we decide what to do.

PERCY   That was a living person.

DEVON   Percy, it's just until we know what we're going to do. And we start off around the mill.

PERCY   Rattle, rattle, rattle.

DEVON   Around the bend.

PERCY   Rattle, rattle, rattle.

DEVON   Across the bridge.

PERCY   Rattle, rattle, clunk.

DEVON   Oh.

PERCY   And Devon picks up the skull from the ground.

DEVON   Sorry. Across the lawn, and into the house. Down the hall and down the stairs.

DEVON exits stage right, bones in hand.

PERCY   Behind the stairs and behind the wood.

DEVON re-enters hands empty.

DEVON   Up the stairs and into the light. Where's the key?

PERCY   Key in my hand, key in the hole. Locked. Where are you going?

DEVON   I need to think.

PERCY   Devon. It had to be some kind of mistake.

DEVON   I'm sure it was.

PERCY   And he turns and walks away.

DEVON gets into bed. He mumbles.

DEVON   I'm sure it was. I'm sure it was.

PERCY gets into bed.

I'm sure it was. I'm sure it was.

PERCY   Devon keeps sighing and talking in his sleep.

DEVON   The bed keeps squeaking, she's been tossing and turning all night.

PERCY   It's too hot tonight, the room has no air.

DEVON   Bones in the basement, bones under the stairs. Bones in my head when I close my eyes.

PERCY   Squeak, creak. Devon sits up, trying to be quiet.

DEVON   "Devon, what's wrong?" She says.

PERCY   "Nothing, just having a little trouble falling asleep." He says.

DEVON   "Would you open the window? It's stuffy in here."

PERCY   "Of course. I'm just going to go downstairs and get a drink of water." His feet padding to the window.

DEVON   "Thank you." From the bed. I tiptoe down the stairs.

   DEVON crosses stage right.

PERCY   I close my eyes and think about falling asleep.

DEVON   Moonlight in the hall.

PERCY   We bury the bones in a new place and forget this day ever happened.

   DEVON stands staring off stage right.

DEVON   The door swings open, staring down the stairs, staring into black.

PERCY   I am on Centre Street. The entire town is standing before me, facing a tall wooden platform. An aisle runs up the middle of the crowd and I walk up it. As I turn my head to the right… to the left… nobody looks at me. Their eyes are locked forward, waiting, waiting for something solemn… sacred. As I advance, I recognize them… Reverend Mueller, the Calvinist minister… Mary Cameron, the baker's wife… Walter Agum, the shoemaker… I am standing before them, their eyes are trained on me. And they begin to move forward, forming a circle… which surrounds me…. A skirt brushes my leg… it tickles, a young hand grazes my shoulder. Mr. Price gives me a squeeze. Closer and closer. I am on the platform. Something scratchy and rough is placed around my neck… I want to take it off but my hands are pinned to my sides as the crowd presses into me. The crowd is gone. No floor beneath me, rope wrapped around my neck, I look down into the cold unfeeling eyes… of the Railrider.

The Railrider, PERCY and DEVON sing a haunting hymn in the round. PERCY crosses to stage left where she burnt the book.

DEVON   The morning.

PERCY   A groggy morning. I want to have a service for the bones… you and I.

DEVON   Alright.

PERCY   And then we can burn them in the furnace at the mill.

PERCY crosses stage left.

Over to the cupboard to find some words for a service.

DEVON   Down the stairs where we keep the wood.

DEVON exits stage right.

PERCY   Metal box from the shelf, a box full of prayers.

DEVON enters.

DEVON   A bundle in my hand. Percy? Are you ready?

PERCY   Down the stairs. Box in hand. Yes.

They cross to each other.

BOTH   Over the bridge, around the bed, and into the mill.

Liar

by Brian Drader

Premiered at Prairie Theatre Exchange, Winnipeg, 2004

Script available from Scirocco Drama

•

Sherri's estranged brother, Jeremy, fell to his death from a rooftop
while in the company of Mark, a drifter, who has since insinuated
himself into Sherri and her husband Ben's lives.
Ben and Sherri's son, Nathan, disappeared seven years ago when
he was five, after Ben was late picking him up from school.

•

> *SHERRI is getting ready for bed. BEN is fiddling with a digital
> camcorder on a tripod.*

SHERRI   He said it was the battery.

BEN   There's nothing wrong with the battery. The light's green. There's
juice. You're sure that's all he said?

SHERRI   Of course I'm sure.

BEN   It probably just needed a cleaning or some stupid little thing like
that, they get their hands on it and they sabotage it, they screw it up
on purpose so you have to keep bringing it back. That's what they do.
Everybody knows it. It's how they make their money.

SHERRI   I didn't take it in.

> *Silence.*

BEN   Why not.

SHERRI   I don't like it when you tape us.

BEN   Why? What's the big deal?

SHERRI   Why do you do it?

BEN   Why didn't you tell me you didn't like it?

SHERRI   Because you liked it. What do you get out of it?

BEN   Look, it's no big deal. If you don't / want to…

SHERRI   / I want to know.

BEN   Forget it, okay? It's no big deal. I'll put it away. Done. Finished.

> *BEN starts dismantling the camera, glancing at SHERRI, trying to read her.*

Hey, did I tell you we got another shot at the Marsh Oil contract? I thought we'd lost them for sure then I blew them off for Jeremy's… well, when Jeremy… anyway, I guess they really liked our package, they still want / to meet.

SHERRI   / I want to have another baby.

> *Silence.*

I just want to talk about it.

BEN   This is coming from him, isn't it?

SHERRI   Ben…

BEN   We haven't talked about it in years, and all of a sudden he's digging around, and you're bringing it up again. What. Is this a team thing? Did you guys work out some kind of plan?

SHERRI   Who cares where it's coming / from.

BEN   / First you invite him to live / with us…

SHERRI   / He didn't have any place to go, and I thought you'd like having him around.

BEN   Yeah, well, I wish you'd quit thinking for me. I'm perfectly capable of thinking / for myself.

SHERRI   / It's just for a few days, maybe a week, until he finds / a place.

BEN   / You told him about Nathan, didn't you? You told him about Nathan, and the two of you got to talking, and the next thing you know you want to have another baby. And you can sit there and look me in the eye and tell me this isn't coming from him?

SHERRI   It doesn't matter where it's coming from. It's here. I'm thinking about it, and I want to talk about it.

BEN   So talk.

SHERRI   I know what it does to you. But what happened is not going to go away. It'll always be there. We can have a dozen kids, or we could split up and never see each other again. It'll still be there. No matter what we do.

BEN   It's not that simple.

SHERRI   Yes it is that / simple.

BEN   / No, it's not!

SHERRI   Shhh!

BEN   I could give a flying fuck if he hears us! Jesus, Sherri. Don't do that. Don't write me off like that, like you know what's best for me, like whatever I'm thinking or feeling is all wrong and it's just a matter of sweeping it aside and setting me straight. It is not that simple. What, you think I've fooled myself into thinking that if we don't have kids I'll get over Nathan? That this is all some big strategy to avoid it, to forget about it? I think about him every day. Sometimes it's just a little smile from a kid at the corner store, and sometimes it's a fucking tornado, all day long, a relentless head on fucking hurricane that's there when I wake up and it's there when I go to bed. You think I don't want to have another kid because he would remind me of Nathan? It's not possible. There is nothing, there is simply nothing that could make me think about him more than I already do.

SHERRI   Then we have another one to forget him. We have a child so we can move on. We have a child for us. To save us.

BEN   I wasn't aware that we required "saving." I actually thought we were doing quite well under the circumstances.

SHERRI   We're not.

BEN   I see.

SHERRI   I'm not happy. I haven't been happy for a long time. Neither have you.

BEN   Don't tell me / what I'm…

SHERRI   / You're not happy! I remember what you were like when you were happy. Whatever has been going on for the last seven years, it is certainly not "happy." You've changed, Ben. You're not the man I married. I don't know who you are. I don't even know where to look. And I'm sick of it. I can't do it anymore.

BEN   So don't. Don't do it anymore. Pack it in. Get on with it. What's stopping you.

SHERRI   You are. I don't want to lose you. But I don't want to waste any more time, either. That's all it is. It's that simple. If I knew this was all going to work out, I would have limitless strength. Limitless patience. I would be able to do whatever it took. Effortlessly. But I don't know that it's going to work out. We might be wasting our time. That's what scares me.

BEN   What scares you is that I might leave, and then you wouldn't have anyone left to blame for this whole fucked up mess.

SHERRI   I have never blamed you for Nathan. I have never done that. How dare you say that to me.

BEN   You don't say it out loud. You're too smart to say it out loud. But it's there. It's been there from the day he disappeared. You think I changed? Look at yourself. I didn't change. I adjusted. I had no choice. He was gone, and it was all about you. Your little boy. Your loss. Your pain. You locked me out, and you blamed me with every breath. With every look, with every gesture you / blamed me.

SHERRI   / That is not / true!

BEN   / You don't even know when you're doing it! We used to go for walks, Sherri. Now I go for a walk so you can have some time for yourself. We used to bathe together, and now you lock the door. You change the sheets after we make love, like we've done something dirty, something you want to forget. You've built this invisible cage around yourself, this moat filled with hurt and blame and I've been shut. Out.

No trespassing. No one allowed in. And *I'm* sick of it. Me. I wish we'd never had Nathan. I wish we'd never met.

A long silence.

When I watch us make love, I see us. Just us. All this crap, all this, it's gone. It doesn't exist anymore. It's just you and me. Like it used to be.

BEN leaves.

Sky

by Connie Gault

Premiered at the Twenty-Fifth Street Theatre Centre, Saskatoon, 1989

Script available from the Playwrights Guild of Canada

•

"In the Sight of God"

The play is set in 1920, in Saskatchewan. This is the first day of a marriage between two young people. It was arranged by the church in an attempt to deal with the two problems—Jasper and Blanche—with one solution.

•

JASPER   Come on in. What do you think eh? It's small, but.... This is the kitchen. And here's the bedroom. Here's the linoleum I was telling you about. I had to nail down the edges. See all the nails? Couldn't have you tripping I said to Mr. Currie, them edges all curl up. I like the linoleum fine, but them edges all curl up and he said, "You can't have that Jasper." He said you've got to nail it down. So I did. *(pause)* Oh. Nearly forgot. Got some money for you. Here. *(pause)*

> *BLANCHE refuses to touch the money. JASPER sets the roll of bills on the table. BLANCHE looks at it. She turns the wedding ring on her finger.*

You can get some material and make curtains.

BLANCHE   *(quietly)* Keep it.

JASPER   No. It's for you. For curtains. Nothing brightens up a house like curtains. That's what Aunt Nell says.

BLANCHE   You keep the money. *(pause)* You're the man in the house, aren't you?

JASPER   Yeah. *(pause)* I was going to buy new curtains, but Aunt Nell said you might like to choose your own.

BLANCHE   I don't give a god-damn about curtains.

JASPER   I know what you want. *(pause)* You want a new dress. *(pause)* Aunt Nell thought you might like a new dress.

BLANCHE   *(after a moment)* God-damn it.

JASPER   What do you want then eh?

BLANCHE   *(after a moment)* Nothing.

JASPER   Sure you do. *(He waits, but not long enough for BLANCHE to decide to speak.)* Well?

BLANCHE   How about some coffee?

JASPER   Coffee? All right. Coffee. Yes sir.

> *JASPER reheats coffee. He begins to hum "What a Friend We Have in Jesus" (lyrics by Joseph Scriven, music by Charles Converse).*

BLANCHE   *(after a few bars)* It could be real quiet here. I'll say that much for this place.

JASPER   It's pretty clean too, eh? Mother was always a stickler for a clean house. I've been working on it all week.

BLANCHE   It's cleaner than the place I left.

JASPER   I figured you'd be surprised. You are surprised, aren't you? You think you're gonna like it?

BLANCHE   Can't tell, can I? Can you cook?

JASPER   Yup.

BLANCHE   Good.

> *JASPER starts humming again.*

JASPER   I guess your family will be coming to visit once we're settled eh? Blanche?

BLANCHE   I don't expect they will.

JASPER   Won't they want to see you? See how you're doing here? Get a look at the house?

BLANCHE   Do you talk all the time?

JASPER   Sorry. But, won't they?

BLANCHE   Naw.

JASPER   But, your mother will worry about you.

BLANCHE   There's mothers and there's mothers.

> *BLANCHE sits in the rocker.*

JASPER   That's Mother's rocker. You— *(pause)* You can sit though. *(pause)* Aunt Nell says it takes some getting used to, being married, but we'll do just fine. I was surprised your family didn't come to the ceremony. Blanche? I said I was surprised your family didn't come to the ceremony.

> *BLANCHE doesn't respond.*

What was your favourite part?

BLANCHE   What?

JASPER   What was your favourite part of the ceremony? Mine was the beginning, just after I saw you standing there waiting for me. Remember, I went and stood beside you, and Reverend Poole started talking. Dearly beloved—we are gathered here together—

BLANCHE   *(interrupting)* I'm sick to death of all this god-damn talking. Why don't you bring me some of that coffee? It must be ready by now, for Christ's sake.

> *JASPER goes to the stove to check on the coffee. He hums "What a Friend We Have in Jesus."*

You do a lot of that?

JASPER   Huh?

BLANCHE   Nothing.

> *JASPER brings the coffee to the table.*

JASPER   You know, I can't stop talking at you. Aunt Nell said it would take some getting used to. She said it might be kind of frightening for you—being married. It might be all—kind of new to you. *(pause)* It's all kind of new to me.

> *JASPER starts humming again as he shovels four or five teaspoonfuls of sugar into his coffee.*

BLANCHE   Did your mother let you do that?

JASPER   Naw.

BLANCHE   That's one nice thing about her being dead eh?

JASPER   You shouldn't say that.

BLANCHE   It's true, ain't it?

JASPER   No. She wasn't even sick. She was making pies and then I went out and when I came back [she was...]

JASPER   She's in heaven now. [where she belongs]

BLANCHE   Well it won't hurt her, what I say then, will it. Since [she's in heaven where she belongs?]

JASPER   You shouldn't talk like that.

BLANCHE   Oh. Well. You listen [here a minute.]

JASPER   You'd better watch what you say [around here.]

BLANCHE   Listen. If I've got to watch every god-damn word that comes out of my god-damn mouth, I might as well just up and leave right now.

JASPER   No.

> *JASPER reaches out to touch her.*

BLANCHE   Don't. Don't you touch me. Do you hear me? Who do you think you are?

> *Silence.*

Don't do it again.

> *Silence.*

Just—drink your coffee.

JASPER drinks his coffee.

Now. You and me have to get a few things straight.

JASPER   Don't you worry. Everything's going to be just fine. *(pause)* You look pretty from the side. *(pause)* Did you ever feel God's hand on your head?

Silence.

BLANCHE   Didn't they tell you anything about me?

JASPER   Not much. What did they tell you? About me?

BLANCHE   Nothing. *(pause)* They didn't tell you I'm pregnant?

JASPER stares. OLD BLANCHE looks through the wall of the house, watching BLANCHE.

Didn't they tell you that?

JASPER   No.

BLANCHE   *(after a moment)* Well, I'm going to have a baby—at Christmas. *(pause)*

JASPER   At Christmas. Well.

BLANCHE   There's more, too. *(pause)*

JASPER   Yeah?

BLANCHE   Yeah. You saying did I ever feel like God's hand was on my head—it made me think I should tell you. *(pause)* It's God's baby. This is God's child I'm having. *(pause)* And don't go blabbing that all over town.

JASPER   No. I won't.

Silence.

BLANCHE   You said yourself you could feel God watching us, today, in the church.

JASPER   Yeah, that's right. When Reverend Poole said, in the sight of God. But—

BLANCHE   *(interrupting)* Forget it.

>   *JASPER reaches out to touch her.*

(quietly) Don't do that.

JASPER   I'm sorry.

BLANCHE   You can't touch me. You can see that, can't you? *(pause)* You are nothing but a man. You mustn't touch me. After God? *(Pause. She waits for him to think about this.)* You see? You'd get me dirty? *(pause)* Wouldn't you?

>   *Silence.*

You wouldn't want that?

JASPER   No.

BLANCHE   *(after a moment)* Fine. Fine. Are you ever, ever going to touch me?

JASPER   No, I won't.

BLANCHE   Fine.

Belle

by Florence Gibson

Premiered at Factory Theatre, Toronto, 2000

Script available from Playwrights Canada Press

•

"A Train Goes Somewhere"

Belle takes place during the Reconstruction Era of the United States
of America, 1865 to 1870, a time when White women and Black
men were agitating to obtain the vote, silencing Black women in
the ensuing political process. In this scene, Nance Hewitt, a White
suffrage worker, travels with Bowlyn Place, a Black man, on a train
to Cincinnati to speak at a political rally. Bowlyn's wife, Belle, has
stayed behind to make money scrubbing floors.

•

NANCE   *(descending from the podium with an overnight case)* Cincinnati
here we come!

A train whistle blows.

Come on, Bowlyn, our train's pulling out—get in!

They leap on board the moving train.

I got us a private coach for *sprawlin'*.

BOWLYN   *(hesitates)* We—we can't.

NANCE   What?

BOWLYN   They—There'll be a fuckin' coloured car somewhere at the
back.

NANCE   What? Asshole! This is the *north*—they wouldn't dare! The war
is over and all them rules are gone—*we're* making 'em up!

A coach compartment of a train. NANCE closes the door, BOWLYN
sits, hands folded. NANCE sprawls.

I gotta watch you Bowlyn Place. When it comes to moving forward,
you get awful prone to shrinkage.

BOWLYN   Where you come from? To be like this?

NANCE   Me? I don't come from nowhere nomore. You smoke?

BOWLYN   Yes. I mean no.

NANCE   I would. But that's not who I'm working towards being, is it?

BOWLYN   S'pose not.

NANCE   Belle never has to work at being who she is, does she?

BOWLYN   Belle just is.

NANCE   I love Belle.

BOWLYN   *(smiles)* Me too.

NANCE   I love that I can be my whole self with Belle cause most other
places I can't be who I am at all and I hate that about myself: sure wish
I could smoke.

BOWLYN   Ain't nobody watchin'.

NANCE   *(lights up cigarette)* I like talkin' to you. I can tell you my whole
life and you won't flinch. I like that about you.
Know what else I like about you?

BOWLYN   No, I—

NANCE   I like your smell. Yes I do. I like sittin' here beside you 'cause
I like your smell. You don't smell like other men I've known.
Just being myself.
I have been known to take a drink now and again. But I ain't got no
problems with it you understand.

BOWLYN   Surely.

NANCE   You drink?

BOWLYN   Now and then.

NANCE   Here and now?

BOWLYN   Well if that ain't a handy little flask.

NANCE   I acquired it as part of the Temperance Movement. Here.

BOWLYN   *(laughs, drinks)* You sure got your share of alignments.

NANCE   Not no mo'. I'm with you. Right here, alignin' myself right 'long side you. Smokin'. Talkin'. Drinkin'. Together.

BOWLYN   Oh. Well. I—

NANCE   What I'm sayin' is: how come there's compartments? How come we can't love wheresoever we fall—White Black man woman—whatsa matter with that?

BOWLYN   Slow down girl, you gonna beat the train to the station. Belle would say—

NANCE   Belle *would*. *(pause)* Well go on.

BOWLYN   Belle would say, it's a matter of goin' cautious, of placin', careful, where the heart might lie. You don't go layin' it at the feet o' someone whose got tramplin' bones in their shoes. That's what Belle would say.

NANCE   And Belle'd be right.
Take you and me. We're the same. I can feel it, between us, something delicate, rich and strange, between us. You and me. You feel it?

BOWLYN   …What's between you and me is Belle.

NANCE   That's right! Bowlyn Place you are right. You're a man women go crazy for, you know that, you hear me?

BOWLYN   *(laughs)* I'm hearin' you.

NANCE   So you be careful, when love leads you by the collar, and down the path to somethin' more…

BOWLYN   Truly Nance, I—

NANCE   Lets talk about that: fuckin'. Me. Should I fuck? 'Cause men do.

BOWLYN   Fuck you?

NANCE   What I'm meanin' is unmarried men—they do it, so why can't I?

BOWLYN   That's different.

NANCE   Why is it different?

BOWLYN   'Cause they is men.

NANCE   I can do anything a man can do! There ain't no difference.

BOWLYN   Why would ya wanna do what men do? Men does awful things too.

NANCE   Tell ya what I did.

BOWLYN   Why do I feel like I should close my eyes when you tell me this?

NANCE   Lumberjackin'.

BOWLYN   Didn't.

NANCE   Did. Cut off my hair, chewed and spat tobacco. Four months I worked, the work of a man. They never knew. Never felt so good before nor since.

BOWLYN   Them big saws?

NANCE   A woman's strength is in her legs. Out in the forest, a logger can be half a mile from his buddies. With nobody lookin', I'd sit on my hind end and use the muscles in my legs the way they was intended. *(demonstrates)*

BOWLYN   Nance.

NANCE   It's true! Loggin's no big thing,—nor drinkin', nor tellin' filthy jokes—they liked mine best. I could work harder and cuss prettier than any of them sissies what never did a honest day's work. I proved myself a better man than any of them… and they hated me for it.

BOWLYN   They found out?

NANCE   Contract over, we're all goin' home next day. Havin' a big drunk. Best workers gettin' surprise bonuses, *I'm* gettin' the biggest. Up on the loggin' trailer, wad 'a money in my fist, just like a political platform, everybody cheering me, the "little fella." Well I couldn't resist, could

I? Had to say who I was. Wouldn't believe me. So. Ripped open my shirt... proof. *(silence)* That night. Four... I guess four, in the dark. Said I wanted it, said why else show my womanliness to them, what else am I for? What else, what else, what else?...

NANCE beats her breast. BOWLYN takes her hands and stops her. NANCE pulls away. She takes a swig from her flask.

Well I say fuck 'em. Fuck 'em all.

Silence.

BOWLYN   I know it be a awful thing, surely.
I know it seem a deep well, sure to drowning, with no light, no sound, no touch, just perpetual fallin'.
And I know it be leavin' you marked, a place burned, branded, a silent, scarred kernel o' soulless hate. 'Cause you be knowin' now, and you be watchful.
But I also know
it be leavin' you wise, you be
wisdom kissed and knowledge stored.
'Cause you be goin' on from that place, that ain't the place that you be stayin', no,
you won't give to them the right to cloud you out of joy, or let their knowledge take stranglehold and bind.
It ain't a world complete that you be choosin' for yourself, to be thinkin' that all others be the same.
For if we are to come to that, how'm I to move t'ward you?
How'm I to take your hand?

Silence. NANCE takes his hand and puts it on her breast. Kiss.

Unity (1918)

Kevin Kerr

*Premiered at the Vancouver East Cultural Centre, Vancouver,
produced by Touchstone Theatre, 2001*

Script available from Talonbooks

•

"A Prophecy"

Outside in the wheat field belonging to her father, Sissy,
a sixteen-year-old apocalypse enthusiast, has dragged the handsome
and ingenuous Michael (15), away from his work on the threshing
crew in order to share some new ideas that she has brought home
from a trip to Edmonton. It's autumn 1918, many of the town's
men are overseas, and there are distant rumours about a strange
and deadly epidemic that's sweeping westwards.

•

MICHAEL   Ah! See this day? This is a good day!

SISSY   You're cold.

MICHAEL   Am not.

SISSY   You've got goosebumps.

MICHAEL   I love those things! That's just me trying to get out of my skin
and get more of a day like this.

SISSY   You look like a featherless chicken boy. Ready for the oven.

MICHAEL   That makes me hungry. Look at my breath! It's like I'm smoking.

SISSY   Do you want to?

MICHAEL   Want to what?

SISSY   Smoke, chicken boy.

She takes out tobacco and paper.

MICHAEL   There's the old shirt! I've missed you buddy!

SISSY   Leave it off.

MICHAEL   Why? *(sees SISSY is rolling a cigarette)* Hey!

SISSY   You'll stop the day from gettin' in.

MICHAEL   You know, it's really freezing if you're not working. Where did you get that?

SISSY   My dad.

MICHAEL   How do you know how to do that?

SISSY   My dad.

MICHAEL   Your dad lets you smoke?

SISSY   Hey! He wouldn't be a very good dad if he let me smoke.

MICHAEL   Well you're not a very good daughter if you don't listen to your dad.

SISSY   My dad already has a good daughter. And there's a difference between what you're supposed to do and what you should do. Here.

MICHAEL   Huh? What do you do?

SISSY   Just suck on it. It'll warm you up.

MICHAEL   That's not much of a fire. *(takes a drag)* Wow! Thank you! *(gives the cigarette back)*

SISSY   *(taking a drag)* You like it?

MICHAEL   No, it's absolutely terrible—Oh, a fire!

SISSY   What? *(She offers the cigarette again.)*

MICHAEL   That's what we have to do. A big bonfire for Hallowe'en. *(waves off cigarette)* No thanks, I've figured that thing out all at once.

SISSY   I like a big fire too.

MICHAEL   Get some wood, chop it up.

SISSY   Better than that, start it in one of those haystacks. That could be a good fire.

MICHAEL   That's feed, though.

SISSY   You wanna know something?

MICHAEL   From you?

SISSY   Yeah, from me.

MICHAEL   What?

SISSY   I've been reading a book.

MICHAEL   *(picks up his shirt)* That is something.

SISSY   Silly. Don't put that shirt on, I told you.

MICHAEL   It's really cold!

SISSY   Don't! Listen. This book says that—you know in the Bible, at the end, there's the part about when the world ends? Everything is taken away.

MICHAEL   Yeah.

SISSY   This book says that it's going to happen this year.

MICHAEL   This year?

SISSY   This year!

MICHAEL   You're funnier than I thought.

SISSY   But it makes sense. The war. The weather. Strange things happening all around. Bad crops this year.

MICHAEL   Not so bad.

SISSY   Pretty bad though.

MICHAEL   Well, yeah, I guess.

SISSY   Listen. Okay, here. We know that the world has six thousand years. Start to finish. Do you believe that?

MICHAEL   I don't know.

SISSY   It's in the Bible.

MICHAEL   Okay, then.

SISSY   Now, also in the Bible, luckily, someone was smart enough to record how long everyone lived when the world was first made.

MICHAEL   And everyone's nine hundred years old or something.

SISSY   Yeah. Well when you count it all up and the time from then to when Jesus was born you get 4,082.

MICHAEL   Uh huh?

SISSY   So 4,082 years went by before Jesus was born. So if there's only 6,000 years in all, how many left after he was born? Until the end.

MICHAEL   I'm not so good at numbers.

SISSY   *(draws in the dirt)* 6,000 minus 4,082 equals 1,918. 1918. You've got goosebumps again.

MICHAEL   That's 'cause it's freezing.

SISSY   So, are you scared?

MICHAEL   Are you?

SISSY   No.

MICHAEL   How come?

SISSY   I don't know. But I'm not. I'm forming a special club. It allows both boys and girls. And it's the end of the world club.

MICHAEL   What do you get to do in the club?

SISSY   Anything you want.

MICHAEL   The end of the world doesn't scare you?

SISSY   Not if it's this year.

MICHAEL   Why not.

SISSY   Because it means you and I get to be the last people on earth!

She rubs his torso.

MICHAEL   What are you doing?

SISSY   Keeping you inside your skin for a little longer.

She kisses him then quickly stops.

Put your shirt on preacher boy. People will think you're trying to impress me.

Rice Boy

by Sunil Kuruvilla

Premiered at the Yale Repertory Theatre, Connecticut, 2000

Script available from Playwrights Canada Press

·

"Eyes Start to Open"

Tommy, visiting India from Canada, is up in the air, having just climbed a coconut tree for the first time. On the ground, his cousin Tina slides on a cart, her legs useless since birth. The girl teaches the boy to see.

·

TOMMY   Who are you?

TINA   Your cousin.

TOMMY   Your legs are weird.

TINA   They don't work.

TOMMY   I can see everything from up here.

TINA   What do you see?

TOMMY   The Fish Man is riding his bicycle. Some men are pushing a taxi. A boy is running beside a tire, slapping it with a stick.

TINA   What does the river look like?

TOMMY   I don't know. Water.

TINA   No—Look.

TOMMY   It's dirty.

TINA   Keep talking.

TOMMY   Your mother is running to the river. I could slip.

TINA   Go higher.

TOMMY   I've never climbed a tree before. They aren't this big in Canada.

> *TOMMY keeps climbing.*

TINA   Are people swimming?

TOMMY   Some.

TINA   How many? Count.

TOMMY   Four. Four men.

TINA   How far is it from here?

TOMMY   My father is sitting down and covering his face. I think he's crying.

TINA   What else do you see?

TOMMY   I'm tired.

TINA   No. Describe. Keep going. What do the houses look like? Are they different from this one? You can be my eyes. How wide is the road? What do the buses look like? And the trucks? They paint big names on the front, don't they? I've heard them drive by all my life.

TOMMY   You've never seen a truck!

TINA   I've never left this house.

TOMMY   Stupid Girl!

TINA   Read the trucks. Tell me what you see.

> *TOMMY starts to read the names on the trucks.*

TOMMY   Vymol. Raju. Georgie. Simon. Saju. Lisa. I always look for "Tommy" but I haven't found one yet.

TINA   Find "Tina."

TOMMY   There's no "Tina." The trucks have boys names.

TINA   You found "Lisa."

TOMMY   I'll find "Tommy" before I find "Tina." First one wins.

TINA   You could lie. I wouldn't know.

TOMMY   You could trust me.

TINA   That hammering sound. Are the women cutting into trees?

TOMMY   Yes. What are they doing? They're hammering nails and putting up coconut shells.

TINA   They're collecting rubber. It comes from the tree.

TOMMY   Like maple syrup.

TINA   You saw that the last time you were here. You must have. All I see are the rubber trees.

TOMMY   I don't remember the last trip.

TINA   Your mother died. You don't remember that?

TOMMY   I was too little.

TINA   Stupid boy.

TOMMY   I can see the whole world. What can you see?

TINA   Stop talking.

TOMMY   I see the sari store. The water fountain. The post office.

TINA   Stop it.

TOMMY   I see chickens running through the church. I see the powder factory and the butcher shop. What can you see?

TINA   The bottom of your feet.

TOMMY   Can you see the powder factory? Smart girl, what can you see?

TINA   Blood.

TOMMY   Where?

TINA   On the ground. You're dripping.

TOMMY   My nose is bleeding. Get me a Kleenex!

TINA   Get it yourself.

   TINA sits on her cart and rolls herself into the house.

TOMMY   Slide close. I want to drip on your head.

Ugly turtle. Slide away. Straighten your skirt. You almost showed me your legs. I don't want to get sick.

Mary's Wedding

by Stephen Massicotte

Premiered at Alberta Theatre Projects, Calgary, 2002

Script available from Playwrights Canada Press

•

"That's poetry, Mary, not real life."

Mary and Charlie argue about Charlie's desire to join the
cavalry at the outbreak of the First World War.

•

CHARLIE   Did you hear the news?

MARY   Yes, Charlie. Yes, I did. Who hasn't?

CHARLIE   "Germany has declared war on Great Britain…"

MARY   "…and Canada pledged her support by offering troops." That's
what the headlines say. What did they really expect to happen? How
did you get past Mother?

CHARLIE   She let me in, said you were reading in here.

MARY   She invited you in. She's changed her opinion of farm boys and
colonists all of a sudden.

CHARLIE   I think maybe she liked me after all.

MARY   I think she likes you more now that you're going to fight for the
British Empire.

CHARLIE   How do you know I'm going?

MARY   Isn't everybody? That's all they're talking about in town. All the
men in my father's office are signing up together.

CHARLIE   Everyone must do their share.

MARY   Charlie.

CHARLIE   I went to militia camp last summer with my cousin.

MARY   So?

CHARLIE   I can shoot.

MARY   So what? That's what they're all saying at my father's office, but they're all just clerks. They file papers and fill their pens and now they think they're soldiers.

CHARLIE   I can ride.

MARY   I know you can. But you don't have to.

CHARLIE   I want to join the Cavalry. I've always wanted to. Like in "The Charge of the Light Brigade."

MARY   Like in "The Charge of the Light Brigade?" *[by Alfred, Lord Tennyson]* Do you listen to yourself when you speak it. "Not tho' the soldier knew Someone had blunder'd? Into the jaws of Death? Into the mouth of Hell?"

CHARLIE   "When can their glory fade? Honour the charge they made!"

MARY   That's poetry, Charlie, not real life.

CHARLIE   They need men who can ride. I can ride. I love to ride. You know what it's like, Mary. The wind and the sky? Your heart beating faster, louder than the hooves. You remember?

MARY   I just thought…

CHARLIE   What? Tell me.

MARY   I thought that it was us. I thought it was us the wind and the sky, faster and louder than the hooves. If you don't come home I'll die of heartbreak.

CHARLIE   That's poetry, Mary, not real life.

   She turns away. Silence.

   I have to go.

MARY   Then go.

CHARLIE   I want to ask you… if you'll meet me in the barn tonight.

MARY   For what. *(pause)* Why?

CHARLIE   There's something I want to ask you.

MARY   No, I won't. Not if you're going to go…

CHARLIE   But Mary…

MARY   If you are going to go then go. I don't care. I won't stop you.

CHARLIE   Please, meet me in the barn.

MARY   I said go away! *(pause)* GO!

CHARLIE walks away.

Hockey Mom, Hockey Dad
by Michael Melski

Premiered at Café Ole in Halifax, produced by Brou-Ha-Ha Theatre, 1995

Script available from Cape Breton Books

•

A Saturday morning in September. Near the end of a game. As the lights
rise on the section of bleachers, there are two parents near each other:
Donna and Teddy. They are what they appear to be. Two young,
working-class parents, watching their children play minor hockey.

•

> *DONNA is a few rows up from ice level in the bleachers. She is
> a quiet, modestly dressed young woman with pretty, un-made-up
> features. She holds a steel travel mug of coffee with both hands,
> warming them against the cold. Beside her is a newspaper.*
>
> *TEDDY leans over the boards. He is a heavy-set, gregarious man,
> wearing an old hockey jacket. He lives the hockey action with fevered
> enthusiasm and body language, surging and sinking with every shot
> and play.*
>
> *They are aware of each other's presence and proximity, but they don't
> know each other. Some of TEDDY's volume is for DONNA. DONNA
> senses this, and is partly-flattered, partly-unnerved by the attention.
> She regards TEDDY, and the action on ice, with concern.*

TEDDY   …Faceoff! Everybody up! Okay now, take er out. Sticks on the
ice! Heads-up plays, fellas. Only eight minutes left. Big comeback! *Big*
comeback! Can't let these Whalers beat us. Hustle down there, Troy,
hustle for it! Stay left wing! Left! *(pause)* Troy! Ya wiener! Do ya know
right from left or what? Jeez! Left! LEFT! It's the hand ya wipe your

nose with! *(pause)* Ryan! Ya gotta go help my son. He's your man in the corner, Ryan! Fight him for it… OWWW! Now what was that now?!

A whistle blows.

Alright! Two minutes for holding! Great call, Ref! I take back what I said about you and your sister. Boys… we got us a power play!

He looks up at the scoreboard.

Okay…. We're down by six and there's seven minutes left. Youse don't worry about that. Youse can still do it. That's… less than a goal a minute.

A buzzer sounds.

Okay! Change em up. Fresh legs, fellas. Let's go.

DONNA   Let's go, you guys.

> *TEDDY sits down near her. He grins, tries to be nonchalant about it, but he's nervous as hell.*

TEDDY   Looks like this one's a lost cause. Oh and Three. I think we got a losin streak on our hands.

> *DONNA smiles tightly. He thrusts his arm at her. She starts.*

I'm Teddy. I'm the loud guy ya always hear over there.

DONNA   Yeah. You are.

TEDDY   I thought I'd come sit over here today. See if the view was any better… here. So what do ya think?

DONNA   Of what.

TEDDY   The game. What do ya think of the game?

> *On the ice, a whistle blows. Play resumes.*

> *DONNA searches for something to say.*

DONNA   I don't think they should penalize the kids for holding. It'd be a lot nicer game if the players held each other more often.

TEDDY   Yeah? That's very… interestin. Hmm. What's your name?

> *He offers his hand again. She takes it, uneasy.*

DONNA   Donna.

TEDDY   Hey. Donna. That's a pretty name.

DONNA   Thanks. *(at a loss)* My mother picked it.

TEDDY   I know it probly sounds like I'm hard on Troy. But ya gotta stay on him. The team gets down. He gives up too easy. He shouldn't give up so easy. He's a lot like his mother that way. My ex-wife. *(pause)* Let's go guys! Not much of a power play!

DONNA   Go Leafs…

TEDDY   *(laughs)* Well, they aren't gonna hear that from way over here, are they?

> *She shrinks. Her next cheer is even smaller.*

DONNA   Go Leafs…

TEDDY   So, uh… why do ya always sit by yourself? Past three weeks, ya been sittin by yourself, over here in no man's land.

DONNA   I don't know any a the other parents.

TEDDY   Well, if ya want to get to know the people in China, ya can't go sittin in Norway!

DONNA   Scuse me…?

TEDDY   So is… ah… your husband not into the hockey?

DONNA   I'm… I'm not married. I don't have a husband.

TEDDY   Oh yeah. Ya don't say. Me neither. I don't got a husband either. *(laughs)* I mean… well, you know what I mean. *(pause)* Right…?

> *DONNA nods, focuses on the game, uncertain of his company, and hesitant with his personal questions.*

DONNA   Let's go Leafs! C'mon.

TEDDY   *(shouts)* C'mon Leafs! Leafs Leafs Leafs Leafs Leafs!

DONNA   C'mon guys. You can do it.

TEDDY   So, which one a all these is yours?

> *Pause.*

DONNA   Matthew. He's number four.

TEDDY   Oh! Number *four*. *(dread)* So *you're* the one who owns number four!

DONNA   He's just a beginner. This is his first year playin.

TEDDY   Yeah. I noticed him. So your boy's a rookie, eh?

DONNA   He just started a new school. I guess he's tryin to fit in. All the other kids were playin.

TEDDY   So then, ya just moved to the island, huh? Where from?

DONNA   Uh. Away.

TEDDY   *(laughs)* Well, that narrows it down.

DONNA   Sorry. I can't… I'm talkin too much. I never talk this much.

TEDDY   Jeez. That's a lot, then.

   She returns to the game.

   C'mon. Don't go stoppin now. *(pause)* You're a quiet one. What are ya so nervous about?

DONNA   *(nervous)* I'm not nervous.

TEDDY   Okay. Okay.

DONNA   I'm just a little worried. About my kid. Y'know? I hope he can take care a himself out there. He's quiet. He's…

TEDDY   Y'know? What he needs is to put on more weight.

DONNA   *(taken aback)* Matthew's weight is normal for a boy his age. His weight is normal.

TEDDY   Sure, maybe it's normal for a boy his age who's takin piano lessons. But it's *not* normal for a boy his age who's a *defenceman*. Defencemen gotta stand up to forwards. They're tough.

DONNA   "Tough." Well, I guess I don't know much about that. I'm only his mother.

   A whistle.

   TEDDY realizes he slipped.

TEDDY   He's got good instincts though. Very good instincts for defence.

Pause.

DONNA   He does?

TEDDY   Oh yeah. Your Matthew? A lotta potential.

DONNA   How?

TEDDY   *(carefully)* Well… he can skate backward… a few feet. He knows how to… ah… fall down in front of shots. Very important in a blueliner. Maybe he shouldn't stay down quite so long, but…. Yeah I can see. The potential in him.

DONNA   *(beaming)* Ya can. Really. No kiddin?

TEDDY   Yeah. Definitely. I can see potential.

TEDDY, undone by her smile, sees potential with her too.

The Anger in Ernest and Ernestine
by Robert Morgan, Martha Ross & Leah Cherniak

*Premiered at the Poor Alex Theatre, Toronto,
produced by Theatre Columbus, 1987*

Script available from Playwrights Canada Press

•

"Bastards!"

•

ERNEST   It was awful.

ERNESTINE   It was really awful Ernest! We came this close. Did your life pass in front of you?

ERNEST   Just the ugly parts.

ERNESTINE   It was that brick. That brick was the final straw. It came— kkk... *(noise of crash)*

ERNEST   It shouldn't have been there. None of it. It was really, really ugly.

ERNESTINE   Sit down, Ernest.

ERNEST   Sit down, Ernestine. I want you to calm down.

ERNESTINE   *(sitting at the table)* If the highway department would put up their signs like they're supposed to, we would have known it was a one-way street, right? How were we supposed to know it was a one-way street, Ernest? How were we to know?

ERNEST   There was an arrow pointing up. I saw an arrow pointing up.

ERNESTINE   What's that supposed to mean?

ERNEST   It means they botched it Ernestine. All those people, coming out of their homes, yelling mean things at us. They botched it with that arrow sign Ernestine.

ERNESTINE   And that moving van coming down the wrong way, the right way... coming right at us. What choice did we have Ernest? What choice?!

ERNEST   No choice!!

ERNESTINE   I think it was a children's playground we went through. Didn't you see that fence we crashed through?

ERNEST   All I saw was a sign with the shadow of a child running free on a yellow triangle.

ERNESTINE   The highway department. It's just not fair. We could sue them Ernest.

ERNEST   A little child... with little stick legs... little round head...

ERNESTINE   In fact, I think that's what we should do.

> *ERNESTINE goes to the cupboard, takes out a pen and sheet of paper and returns to the table.*

We should write them a letter. *(writing)* Oh, this pen doesn't work.

ERNEST   Don't worry about the pen.

ERNESTINE   I want to write a letter. We have to write a letter! It was this close!

ERNEST   They have no right. It's ludicrous!

ERNESTINE   It's ludicrous what they do out there. The government is ludicrous.

ERNEST   We should write a letter. This pen doesn't work.

ERNESTINE   Don't worry about the pen. Just write it.

ERNEST   To whom it may concern...

ERNESTINE   We were nearly killed.

ERNEST   To whom not "it may." To whom it does concern.

ERNESTINE   To whom it does concern!

ERNEST   And I am going to underline the does!

ERNESTINE   That's good Ernest. *(grabbing the pen and paper and writing)* Underline it three times and put an exclamation mark. We were nearly killed!

ERNEST   To whom it better concern! *(grabbing paper and pen back)*

ERNESTINE   Yeah! To whom it better concern. That's good Ernest.

ERNEST   To whom it damn well better concern!

ERNESTINE   Yeah Ernest! Yeah! Or else!

ERNEST   To whom it *(pausing)* to whom it damn well better concern, or else!!

ERNESTINE   Or fuckin' else, Ernest! Fuckin' else!!

ERNEST   Fuckin' else! To whom it damn well better concern or fuck you!!

ERNESTINE   That's good Ernest! Keep it!!! To whom it fuckin' better concern or fuck off!!!

ERNEST   To whom it… to whom it fuckin' better concern or fuck off… fuck you…

ERNESTINE   Fuck you!

ERNEST   Fuck… fuck off or fuck you?

ERNESTINE   Both!!!

ERNEST   Both. Both!! To whom it fuckin' better concern or both fuck off and fuck you!!!

ERNESTINE   That's good Ernest! That's good. Now what goes next? We were nearly killed…

ERNEST   No. Oh no! You nearly killed us!

ERNESTINE   You did!

ERNEST   You did!

ERNESTINE   You tried to kill us!

ERNEST   You did!

ERNESTINE   You…

ERNEST   You…

ERNESTINE   You…

ERNEST   You bastards!

ERNESTINE   Bastards, that's good Ernest!

ERNEST   Bastards!

ERNESTINE   Bastards!

ERNEST   Bastards!

ERNESTINE   Bastards! Just keep writing Ernest, we don't want to miss any of the details.

ERNEST   Bastards!

ERNESTINE   The bricks…

ERNEST   Bastards!

ERNESTINE   The kids, the fence, the yelling…

ERNEST   You bastards fuck off!!

ERNESTINE   That's good, keep it!!!

ERNEST   *(standing)* You bastards can fuck right off!!!

ERNESTINE   *(standing)* Can fuck right off! You fuckin' bastards can fuckin' fuck right the fuck off!!!

They sit and read to themselves what they've written.

ERNESTINE   To many fuckin's? Ernest, we only have one life to live and they nearly took it away! Write that down.

ERNEST   I will.

ERNESTINE   No. No. *(standing, grabbing the letter and putting it in her purse)* I'm going to tell them. I'm going to go right out there and…

ERNEST   No, don't go out there.

ERNESTINE   I'm going out there because we're sitting here like dodos on a log…

ERNEST   You can't go out there.

ERNESTINE   Ernest, I'm not going to sit here like a dodo on a log.

They collide in front of the table, pushing and shoving like children.

I'm—

ERNEST   You can't—

ERNESTINE   Dodo—

ERNEST   Don't go—

ERNESTINE   I'm not *(gasping, clapping her hand over her mouth and backing away)* Oh Ernest!

ERNEST   What?

ERNESTINE   Your face.

ERNEST   My face?

ERNESTINE   Your face is a bit squished in. The fence it…. You have the imprint of the fence on your face.

ERNEST   *(turning his back to the audience)* Does it look funny? Do I look funny?

ERNESTINE   I still love you, Ernest.

ERNEST   They had no right to put a fence there.

ERNESTINE   Well then you go out there and tell them.

ERNEST   You think I look ugly.

ERNESTINE   You don't look ugly, you just have a face that's a bit squished in.

ERNEST   I have a face that looks like a fence!

ERNESTINE   *(pausing)* Ernest, we could sue them!

ERNEST   Those bastards!

The File

by Greg Nelson

Premiered at the SummerWorks Festival, Toronto, 2005

Script available from www.gregnelson.ca

•

Harry Maclean is a professor of law and future Supreme Court Justice who, in 1981, is helping to draft the Canadian Charter of Rights and Freedoms. Janey Coates is an investigative reporter, and an old friend. She has uncovered an explosive scandal: the Minister of Justice, the Honourable William Thorpe, has connections to organized crime. If it comes out, Thorpe is finished. And so is the Charter of Rights and Freedoms.

•

> *The past. HARRY and JANE.*

> *JANE has the mini-cassette recorder. The file sits on the table, in front of HARRY.*

JANE   It's just going to be you?

HARRY   Yes.

> *JANE places the recorder on the table between then, presses record. HARRY watches her. He is pale, tense.*

JANE   *(for the tape)* I'm at Justice in Ottawa with Harry Maclean. *(to HARRY)* How do you want to do this? Do you want to talk first? Or should I start? I have a number of questions.

> *HARRY does not respond.*

Harry?

> *Again, HARRY does not respond. He looks a bit nauseous. JANE watches him, patient.*

Still nothing.

Okay, why don't—

HARRY   I'm missing the party.

JANE   I'm sorry?

HARRY   The birthday party. The dinner, for Adam.

JANE   That's tonight?

HARRY   Yeah. Elaine made a cake.

He pauses. JANE watches him.

I keep telling myself, he's no different. He's just one day older. But it's…. It's more than that, it just is. It's a milestone.

JANE   Thirteen.

HARRY   He's crossing over. He's leaving childhood, and joining us. All day, I've had this thing in my gut, this knot of… what. Fear? Because it's too late, now. He's the most important thing in my world, and I've blown it. I have not done well. I have not… prepared him. Not for this.

JANE watches him. She doesn't know what to say.

JANE   I'm sure that's not true, Harry.

HARRY   What does he see, I wonder? When he looks at me?

A pause. Then HARRY pulls himself together. His face becomes hard.

I'm sorry.

JANE   Don't be.

HARRY   Okay. Let's do this.

JANE   Why don't I start.

HARRY   No, Jane, I'm sorry, you're not going to ask any questions. I'm going to talk. And then you're going back to Toronto.

JANE   Harry, I told you—

HARRY   You're not going to speak with the Minister, ever. It's not going to happen.

A beat. She looks at him.

JANE   You're sure about that?

HARRY   Yes.

JANE   You've talked to Bobby and *whoever* and they agree? That's not a good decision, Harry. No, I mean it. You need to reconsider that, all of you.

HARRY   Jane.

JANE   If you want the story to—

HARRY   You're not going to write the Morelli story.

JANE   *(sighs)* No, Harry, listen—

HARRY   Just let me—

JANE   No! That's not going to work this time—

HARRY   Jane—

JANE   You can't just pick up a phone and—

HARRY   *(intense)* Shut up. Shut the fuck up.

JANE stares at him, shocked. HARRY is sweating, the strain showing through.

I apologize. Please, just let me do this.

He breathes.

Last week, after we met for the first time, after your list of names… I spoke to Bobby. And the two of us spoke, on the phone, to the Minister. They were extremely concerned. They had a number of, in my opinion, reckless ideas on how to respond. They were panicking. We argued at some length. Eventually, I was able to convince them that I could… fix it. I could make it go away. And so, as you know, I made a phone call to Charlie. To your editor.

He pauses. He breathes.

Today, after our second meeting, and your second set of… revelations… again, I spoke to Bobby and to the Minister. Again we argued. I told them: we have worked too hard. And the work is too important. We simply cannot let this get in the way.

He looks at her. She waits.

I won the argument, Jane. What's about to happen… was my idea.

He opens the file. He takes out a large envelope.

As of approximately two o'clock this afternoon, you have been placed under… surveillance.

JANE looks at him. Then she smiles. HARRY doesn't.

JANE   You're kidding.

She smiles again.

Could you say that again?

HARRY   You're under surveillance.

JANE   Harry, do you have any idea how ridiculous that sounds? I'm under *surveillance*? By who?

No answer.

Harry—

HARRY   You and your family.

This instantly stops her smile.

JANE   I'm sorry?

HARRY   You and your family are under surveillance.

JANE   Do you…. Are you talking about my children?

HARRY doesn't answer. She stares at him. He takes a photograph out of the envelope.

HARRY   This is a photo of your two daughters, at the playground across from your home in Toronto. It was taken earlier today. About six hours ago.

JANE is stunned. She stares at the photo.

JANE   *(quiet)* Oh my God. Oh my God.

She stares at the photo. Then she looks up at him.

HARRY stares back at her, silent. He can't believe this is happening either. That he is doing this. Saying this.

HARRY   You will abandon the story. You will give us all of your research and your notes. You will never speak about it, to anyone. If you already have, you will find a way to convince them that you have made an error. That you were mistaken. If you do this…

Again, he breathes.

You will not lose custody of your children. And they will not come to…

He can't continue. She is staring at him, calm now.

JANE   To what. To what, Harry. Say it.

HARRY   To harm.

A long pause. Silence.

Then, JANE reaches over to the mini-cassette. She shuts it off. She gives the recorder to HARRY. He takes it. She closes her notebook, pushes it across the table to him.

Jane? I'm sorry.

They gaze at each other.

Therac 25

by Adam Pettle

Premiered at the Atlantic Theatre Festival, Halifax, 1995

Script available from Scirocco Drama

•

Moira is lying on a treatment cot waiting to be administered her
daily dose of chemotherapy. There is an IV bag hanging beside her,
but she is not hooked up yet. She is reading a *National Enquirer*
magazine. Alan, who is also a cancer patient, enters dressed in
a surgical mask, gloves, stethoscope, and lab coat.

•

ALAN   *(putting on a latex glove and doing his best mad German doctor
impersonation)* Moira! Moira!

MOIRA   *(putting paper down)* What are you doing here?

ALAN   The woman at Patient Information told me your chemo was in
here.

MOIRA   She shouldn't have.

ALAN   What are you reading?

MOIRA   *King Lear.*

ALAN   Really? I didn't know Burt Reynolds was in that one.

MOIRA   What are you doing here?

ALAN   I haven't seen you in a few days. I… I thought I could keep you
company.

MOIRA   This is not really a company thing.

ALAN   Oh. Do you want me to leave?

MOIRA   I'm still deciding.

ALAN   Have your had your…. Sorry, I don't know how this works.

MOIRA   They have to test my blood to make sure it's okay to poison it.

ALAN   Right. What are we having today, anyway?

MOIRA   It's a lovely zinc flan, not currently on the menu.

ALAN   Special.

MOIRA   Yes. And you?

ALAN   No thanks, I ate.

MOIRA   No, I mean have you had your treatment yet?

ALAN   Yeah, I just came from there.

MOIRA   How was it?

ALAN   Oh Christ, you missed quite the rhubarb this morning.

MOIRA   Rhubarb?

ALAN   Well, there was almost a fight in the waiting room.

MOIRA   Fuck off.

ALAN   I swear to God.

MOIRA   Between?

ALAN   Between the praying mantis and the—

MOIRA   The praying mantis?

ALAN   You know, the forty-something Portuguese woman who sits in the corner and prays out loud until she's called in?

MOIRA   I know the one.

ALAN   Well, it was between her and the nose.

MOIRA   The nose?

ALAN   *(bending his nose)* The nose.

MOIRA   Not her!

ALAN   Yes, see the mantis was sitting in the corner praying as per usual, y'know, Portuguese Hail Marys out loud, interrupted by only the occasional moan. You know the drill?

MOIRA   Yes.

ALAN   And so in walks the nose, and she's... she's visibly upset.

MOIRA   I can't see why.

ALAN   No, I know. The woman's on like week four of having her nose burnt off, needless to say she doesn't have much patience. So, she sits down like two seats away from the mantis, because—between you and me—I think she's been wanting to get into it with her for a while. Anyway, she lasts about ten seconds until she leans over and goes: "Will you do us all a giant favour and please SHUT THE FUCK UP!"

MOIRA   No.

ALAN   Yeah, and the mantis stands up, not missing a beat, and goes: "You can pick your friends, and you can pick your nose, but—"

MOIRA   (*laughing*) You are so full of shit.

ALAN   Okay, it was slightly embellished. Do you mind if I... just hang out for a bit?

MOIRA   If you want to. All right.

> *ALAN takes off the stolen hospital garb and stuffs it under MOIRA's cot.*

MOIRA   So, how's the circuit treating you?

ALAN   The circuit?

MOIRA   The eel-wrestling circuit.

ALAN   You know, for someone who doesn't partake, you seem to know more than a few allegories to describe—

MOIRA   Allegories?

ALAN   What? Is that the wrong word?

MOIRA   Dante's representation of hell in *The Divine Comedy* is an allegory, wrestling the eel is not.

ALAN   What is it, then?

MOIRA   A sin. *(pause)* So, I thought you were avoiding me.

ALAN   No, why?

MOIRA   Well, it's just… I haven't seen you in a week.

ALAN   I know; I've had really early appointments.

MOIRA   Oh. I thought maybe maybe you didn't want to hang around with someone who… who watches Montel.

ALAN   We all have our vices.

MOIRA   Yeah, and you've got a vice grip on your—

ALAN   Oh, y'know, can we please just let that die?

MOIRA   Actually, that's not the best allegory to use in here.

ALAN   I'm sorry. *(pause)* So can we?

MOIRA   Can we what?

ALAN   Drop the masturbation thing?

MOIRA   Absolutely not.

ALAN   Thank you.

MOIRA   I've got to have something on you.

ALAN   Why?

MOIRA   Why? Because you caught me reading the *National Enquirer* and because…

ALAN   Because?

MOIRA   I don't let people in here.

ALAN   Oh.

MOIRA   Well, don't get smug.

ALAN   I'm not smug.

MOIRA   Just… don't. Where are they?

ALAN   Who comes in to give you the—?

MOIRA   You know, I really don't feel like talking any more.

ALAN   Oh. Okay. Do you want me to leave?

MOIRA   No. Just... sit there and keep me company, okay?

ALAN   Okay.

Private Jokes, Public Places
by Oren Safdie

Premiered at Malibu Stage Company, California, 2001

Script available from Playwrights Canada Press

.

"Interrogation"

A young Korean student presents a public swimming pool as her final
thesis to a jury of world famous architects. After an hour of back and
forth about Margaret's project, the jurors have grown frustrated with
Margaret's inability to allow them to define her work and move on to the
next project. She simply won't allow them to define her pool as part of
any style, ism, type, or movement. Erhardt decides to change tactics.

.

ERHARDT   *(an idea)* I know! Perhaps we should approach this in
a different way. Let's turn things around. You be the critic for the
moment. In fact, here... take my chair. *(He gets up and offers his seat
to MARGARET.)* There...

   MARGARET takes the stand.

(approaching her like a prosecutor) Now, tell us what you see.... Try to
be critical.

MARGARET   Of my own project?

ERHARDT   Yes.

   She looks at it for a moment.

MARGARET   I think it's very good.

ERHARDT   You mean to say there's nothing wrong with it?

MARGARET   Not that I can see.

ERHARDT   So you think it's perfect?

MARGARET   No. But at this precise moment I am unable to see any flaws.

ERHARDT   Nevertheless, you admit there might be flaws.

MARGARET   Not necessarily.

ERHARDT   And what about the other projects in the room?

MARGARET   I'd rather not discuss them.

ERHARDT   Just say whatever comes to mind.

MARGARET   I don't feel comfortable criticizing my classmates' work.

ERHARDT   Of course not! You would feel awkward criticizing their work because…?

MARGARET   They're my friends.

ERHARDT   Good friends?

MARGARET   Some of us have become close.

ERHARDT   And yet when you look around this room, is there one project that stands out from the rest? Or to quote a famous American children's show, which one of these is not like the others?

MARGARET   My project is somewhat different.

ERHARDT   Very different?

MARGARET   Different.

ERHARDT   So, you're not willing to criticize your classmates' projects to their faces, but isn't that what you're doing by presenting this model here today?

MARGARET   Not at all.

ERHARDT   I mean by your own admission, you destroyed your previous project—which was quite similar to those in this class—because you felt it was misguided, and isn't that exactly what you're saying to all of us here today, by bringing in this project? That you, somehow, possess a purer knowledge, a keener inkling of what makes for the right solution?

MARGARET   I don't care about what everyone else thinks.

ERHARDT   So, you didn't come to school to learn...

MARGARET   I didn't say that.

ERHARDT   Or perhaps it was to teach?

MARGARET   I came to develop my own opinions.

ERHARDT   And was this school the only one you were accepted to?

MARGARET   No, several others.

ERHARDT   But surely you knew the reputation of this school, and what philosophy it was advocating?

MARGARET   They offered me a scholarship.

ERHARDT   And this is how you return the gesture? By rejecting everything this school stands for. Not to mention putting your professor in a very compromising position.

MARGARET   I don't care. I don't owe anybody anything.

ERHARDT   And you live in a vacuum, confident with your beliefs, unconcerned with what the whole world thinks.

MARGARET   That's right.

ERHARDT is frustrated he is unable to crack MARGARET.

ERHARDT   *(approaching MARGARET again—new strategy)* So, you didn't put any time or effort into your physical appearance here today.

MARGARET   What do you mean?

ERHARDT   Well, there's no sense in denying that you've put yourself together today in a way that makes you look very attractive... even arousing...?

MARGARET   *(taken aback)* Excuse me?

ERHARDT   Perhaps it might even have influence on the way we, the jury, perceive your project.

MARGARET   That's not *my* problem.

ERHARDT   Nevertheless, by choosing a certain style, electing to wear those square-toed shoes with high heels, these are obviously not a choice made for reasons of comfort, as such a shape hardly conforms to the contour of your foot. And wouldn't you know it, as I look around this room I notice similar footwear on many of your female classmates, and even some of the males.

MARGARET   I have to wear clothes.

ERHARDT   Do you? It's a hot day today. You're nervous. Even perspiring. *(accusingly)* Wouldn't it make more sense for you to take your clothes off and stand before us in something more functional?!

MARGARET   *(proudly)* I dress the way I feel.

ERHARDT   Nevertheless, you wear clothing! And very stylish clothing I may add. Therefore, there is a part of you that is capable of conforming. It's evident in your dress, the way you comb your hair, it's even noticeable in the way you've applied your make-up. *(to the class)* My teenage daughter does her nails in the exact same way. She calls it rainbow style. *(back to MARGARET)* Perhaps even the name, Margaret, is an attempt by your parents to make you feel like you belong in this country. It's hardly very Korean. In effect, whether you like it or not, you are very much an example of conformity. Some years the hems on your skirts will rise, some years they'll fall, but will this have to do with the fluctuation in temperature? I seriously doubt it. You will be following a trend which will have been established by numerous psychological factors, such as is there a war? Is there peace? In what fashion the President's wife decides to cut her hair…. Or perhaps you will react against the style and, in effect, try and create your own style, only to find out that others have reacted with you, and once again, you are back in style!!!

MARGARET   *(fighting back)* But architecture isn't about fashion or style. It has to be greater than that. Not only does it have to have relevance today, it has to be relevant tomorrow, even twenty years from now. You can't just put a building away in a closet when it becomes dated.

ERHARDT   That's what makes it so interesting. Our cities are walking museums, filled with different styles of architecture, from different periods, that give us insight to our past as well as providing the seeds for our future. Could a Picasso come up with Cubism if he didn't react against Impressionism? Or to use a hero of yours, do you think Louis Kahn could have imagined the Salk Institute if he didn't have those public housing projects to rebel against?

MARGARET   But those movements used to evolve slowly, over time, responding to new technologies and social needs. *(about ERHARDT)* Not because some young, insecure architect is intent on trying to shock the world so *he* can become the next big sensation!

ERHARDT   *(pressing)* And what you've presented here today has nothing to do with *your* feelings of inadequacy?!

MARGARET   Of course not.

ERHARDT   *Your* need to stand out.

MARGARET   No!

ERHARDT   *Your* need to feel different than everyone else in this room!

MARGARET   I am different!!

ERHARDT   Even superior!!

MARGARET   Yes!!!...

> *MARGARET is exposed. ERHARDT is satisfied that he has gotten his confession.*

That's not what I meant to say...

ERHARDT   *(softly)* You may give me back my chair...

> *MARGARET rises from the chair and staggers away to the back of the class, looking shell-shocked.*

Habitat

by Judith Thompson

Premiered at the Canadian Stage Company, Toronto, 2001

Script available from Playwrights Canada Press

•

Sparkle and Raine are two residents of Lewis' newly opened group
home that has become a bone of contention in the neighbourhood
in which it operates. Here, they discuss their views on how to
behave in a community that doesn't want them

•

*Late at night. RAINE asleep. SPARKLE appears breathless. He opens
his backpack.*

SPARKLE   You were playing Nintendo with me all night, okay? We were
playing "Dark Rhapsody" and I fell asleep and you were watching me
sleep…

RAINE   What's going on?

SPARKLE opens the sack and spills the contents in front of her.

SPARKLE   BOUNTY, beautiful bounty.

RAINE   What's this?

SPARKLE   Number 459. It was so obvious they're away, blinds down,
newspapers piling up, desperate cat rubbing against my leg.

RAINE   How'd you get in?

SPARKLE   Through the mailbox, I'm a shapeshifter.

RAINE   Sparkle. You BROKE into a HOUSE.

SPARKLE   Look! A silver fork! An actual sterling silver fork! And a knife!
and a spoon and two five-dollar bills and even, even, a teenaged girly

girls diary!!! "my mother is so incredibly lame she was wearing knee socks today. I ate two chocolate bars yesterday I am getting so fat Fat fat fat I hate myself." I could get THOUSANDS for this!! I could go on Antiques Road show and and…

RAINE   I can't believe you broke into a house…

SPARKLE   I know, it's so immature. In fact it's babyish. It was so clean the floors smelled like bleach. And they had like sixteen different kinds of crackers just crazy about crackers I guess, and…

RAINE   That's exactly what they expect us to do, Sparkle. Why are you playing into their worst…?

SPARKLE   Because. It's exciting. To go where you aren't supposed to go. To go where you would never EVER be invited. I didn't steal anything expensive, I didn't touch the Rolex watch, or the jewellery, or the new IMAX computer, or the fancy pantsy ART OR the Siamese CAT.

RAINE   You are so weird.

SPARKLE   Gonna turn me in?

RAINE   …no.

SPARKLE   Because I would drown myself in the sink before I go back to jail.

RAINE   Don't worry.

SPARKLE   Harry and Doreen are RUTHLESS with squealers, you should have SEEN what they did to little DAVID over at Parkdale? Drove him out to the zoo in the middle of the night, and threw him in naked with the Siberian tigers, I am serious, the tiger mauled him almost to death he only has one hand now, it was all over the news—they are really rough people, though, don't you find? Have you watched the way Doreen eats?

RAINE   Every time we're in the same room she says "what are you looking at?" I don't think she likes me.

SPARKLE   She hates you, she told me.

RAINE   Promise me you won't do that again.

SPARKLE   HAH! You're really hilarious you know that? I mean really really side splittingly hi-larious!! HA HA HA HA HAHAHAHA!!

RAINE   Sparkle! It could be very bad for Lewis. With the neighbours and everything. Very VERY bad. Lewis would be VERY mad at you, you know.

SPARKLE   Ohhhhh "Lewwwiss" is it? It's so obvious you have a big wonking crush on him, the way your voice sort of wavers when you say his name.

RAINE   Mr. Chance? Are you kidding me?

SPARKLE   It's okay, everyone has a crush on him.

RAINE   Well I don't. I think he's an asshole.

SPARKLE   YEAH? If you think he's such an asshole why do you STARE at him?

RAINE   I stare at Mr. Chance?

SPARKLE   You can't take your eyes OFFA him. Anyways, darling, he's taken.

RAINE   He's married?

SPARKLE   *(laughs, hard)* HAHAHA! I think he was, actually, to some shopgirl from New Brunswick with too much lipliner and a name like Sherry Lynn when he was like in HIGH school. But not NOW silly. He has a boyfriend.

RAINE   He's gay.

SPARKLE   Well duh. DOZY HEAD. DUH—

RAINE   Why are you being—so—

SPARKLE   He doesn't like girls. Is that clear?

RAINE   Sparkle. I am not in the LEAST interested in Mr. Chance. It has never OCCURRED to me, actually, and I resent you implying that I…

SPARKLE   Yakety yakety yakety yak. You TALK too much, girlfriend.

   He smokes.

RAINE   I think you're the one with the crush on Mr. Chance.

SPARKLE   Who me? Please. He is totally not my type. He is SO lower middle class. I mean his shoes? Did you happen to notice his shoes?

RAINE   I still think you have a crush on him.

The Ventriloquist

by Larry Tremblay

translated by Keith Turnbull

Premiered at Factory Theatre, Toronto, 2006

Script available from Talonbooks

·

DOCTOR LIMESTONE   Take off your shoes. Take off your shoes. Take off your shoes, Gaby!

GABY   It's in the prospectus?

DOCTOR LIMESTONE   Yes, yes, certainly. *(She imitates taking them off even though she is wearing shoes.)* No! No! No! You must take them off for real! You must take another step. You need certainties. I am offering you the chance to get out of your deep depression. Because you are deeply depressive, are you not? Keep up with me. Take off your shoes, and so, experience the relief. You deserve it. Release yourself! *(She hesitates, pulls herself together, then takes off her shoes.)* Do not forget that everything depends on your capacity to descend into total ignominy. You are just trash, debris. Appreciate our relationship. Without me, you suffer. Admit it. Say it!

GABY   What, Doctor Limestone?

DOCTOR LIMESTONE   Say clearly: without Doctor Limestone, I suffer.

GABY   Without Doctor Limestone, I suffer.

DOCTOR LIMESTONE   Have you found relief by taking off your shoes?

GABY   Yes, at last yes, yes it is undeniable, I think so, no I don't think so, it's more than that, yes I felt a—yes that's it, that's exactly it—a relief, Doctor Limestone.

DOCTOR LIMESTONE   Listen, Gaby, do not play with my nerves. We are at a crucial stage in our therapeutic relationship. When I ask if by taking off your shoes you find relief, answer: yes, Doctor Limestone. Is that clear?

GABY   But that is what I said, Doctor /

DOCTOR LIMESTONE   Go on.

GABY   Yes, Doctor Limestone. I am going on. I take four months to write the most beautiful novel in the world. As soon as I come home from school, I lock myself in my room, plunge the nib of my Parker into the ink well and pump the ink imagining the surge of turquoise waves on the lined pages of my notebooks. The precise moment when I feel the ink rise into the reservoir fills me with a gnashing power. Then my veins inflate and I seem to hear them howling.

DOCTOR LIMESTONE   Ah! Ah!

GABY   What, Doctor Limestone?

DOCTOR LIMESTONE   Pay no attention to me. Go ahead, gallop on.

GABY   I am going ahead, Doctor Limestone. I am galloping on. *(very fast)* Since beginning to write the most beautiful novel in the world, cleanliness becomes secondary. I hardly eat. I no longer go to church on Sunday and, on top of it all, I no longer have any interest in my classmates whom I consider inferior. Even my professors seem like midgets or marionettes. What do they know of the real world? How can they pretend to communicate a vision of the world? From their mouths escape nothing but clichés and pregurgitated ideas. I pity them. They have no idea who is really sitting silently in front of them, impatient to leave their world of banalities and platitudes to regain the vertigo of creation. As soon as I set foot back in my room, gusts of genius tremble through the walls. I take off the ridiculous clothes the school rules force me to wear and I disappear into a thick dressing gown. Then, I open my notebooks. My back bent, my head tilted, my right hand drawn to the Parker which runs after the words escaping from its golden nib, I plunge. Never has a writer written as I have done! After a week, exalted by dozens and dozens of scribbled pages, by the unbridled characters from out of my imagination, I decide to sleep no more. A writer of my calibre goes without sleep. Why lose precious hours in bed when the most beautiful novel in the world is still unfinished? To keep my edge, I drink coffee. I drink an ocean of coffee. Among the innumerable substances which have stayed in or passed through the organs of my body, it is coffee which tops the list for quantity. I am convinced of it. Coffee.

DOCTOR LIMESTONE Coffee. Very good. Very very very good. *(He mumbles something.)*

GABY What are you saying? *(He mumbles again.)* I do not understand, Doctor Limestone. *(He mumbles again.)* I don't understand!

DOCTOR LIMESTONE Take off your dress.

GABY What?

DOCTOR LIMESTONE Take off your dress! And don't try that mime trick on me again. Enough of that!

GABY You are losing your mind, Doctor Limestone!

DOCTOR LIMESTONE The prospectus! Take off your dress!

GABY But I do not see why I /

DOCTOR LIMESTONE So why did you take off your shoes? Why?

GABY Because you asked me to, that's all!

DOCTOR LIMESTONE Then take off your dress when I ask you to!

GABY But there is a difference between shoes and /

DOCTOR LIMESTONE Gaby, I'm counting to three. At three proceed.

GABY What is happening to you?

DOCTOR LIMESTONE One, two, three.

A beat. They stare intensely at each other.

GABY If it's written in the /

DOCTOR LIMESTONE It is written.

GABY takes off her dress.

How do you feel?

GABY   I don't know.

DOCTOR LIMESTONE   The success of my method depends on the strength of conviction that possesses the underwear. That surprises you doesn't it? *(GABY nods her head yes. He exhales loudly.)* Stand up straight. Everything's caving in on you, but don't show it. Stand up straight because everything is caving in on you like the floors of a house which fall one on top of each other from the attic to the cellar. How do you feel?

GABY   I don't know. I don't know anymore.

DOCTOR LIMESTONE   Don't run away from it. Answer my question: how do you feel?

GABY   I have a stomachache. I want to vomit. I wish I could fall through the floor.

DOCTOR LIMESTONE   Aha! Excellent! *(He moves closer to her.)* You have goose bumps. What is underwear? That is the question. I have a story to tell you too. One day, my mother punished me. You know why? I had stolen money from her pig to buy me candies. My mother owned an enormous pig. You know what I mean: a bank shaped like a pig—a piggy bank. I managed to extricate some change from her big pig to buy myself some candy. My mother, a very suspicious person, had noticed it. She tied me to a chair, in my underwear, and made me drink onion soup. I abhor onion soup. I abhor all shapes and forms of onions: in photos, in soups certainly, in salads, in quiches. Onions repulse me. The day when my mother made me swallow—tied to a chair—an entire bowl of onion soup, I understood the strength of conviction of underwear. What is underwear? Answer me! What is underwear?

GABY   I don't know Doctor Limestone. But in fact, yes, of course, I know what underwear is, it is precisely what I am wearing at this very moment but you ask the question in such a way that it is very difficult to answer your /

DOCTOR LIMESTONE   Shut up. *(He touches her with the tips of his fingers.)* Always goosebumps. Why? Are you cold?

GABY   Yes, Doctor Limestone.

DOCTOR LIMESTONE   It's very hot in here. Really very hot. I—I'm very very hot. It's unacceptable, Gaby. I can't bear this contradiction. Not at all at all!

GABY   I don't understand, Doctor Limestone.

DOCTOR LIMESTONE   Call me Bob.

GABY   Bob?

DOCTOR LIMESTONE   Bob. Realize the nothingness you inspire. Sink, Gaby sink down step by step into profound sensations of loss.

GABY   I'm sinking, Doctor Limestone, I'm sinking.

DOCTOR LIMESTONE   Bob. Call me Bob.

GABY   Yes, Bob.

DOCTOR LIMESTONE   D'you like standing in front of Bob in your underwear—you delicate little trash?

GABY   Yes, Bob.

DOCTOR LIMESTONE   How do you feel? Are you still cold?

GABY   No, no, not at all, not at all at all, Bob. I'm very hot.

DOCTOR LIMESTONE   Excellent. What progress, what progress!

Scenes

2 females

The Orphan Muses

by Michel Marc Bouchard

translated by Linda Gaboriau

Premiered at Théâtre Aujourd'hui, Montreal, 1988

Script available from Scirocco Drama

•

Four siblings are reunited in their family home in an isolated
village in Québec. They are awaiting the return of their mother who
abandoned them fifteen years earlier. Isabelle, the youngest daughter,
who has remained at home with Catherine, the oldest sister,
has organized homecoming festivities which will not turn out
to be what her sisters and brother expect.

Martine, stationed with the Canadian Armed Forces in Germany, returns
home for the first time in years. She has been duped by Isabelle who
announced their brother Luc's sudden death in order to bring her back to
Canada. Convinced that Martine never would have come back for their
mother's return, Isabelle fabricated this lie. Their brother is still very much
alive and, hidden, he observes the scene between the two sisters.

•

ISABELLE   *"If at your window you see a gentle dove*
Treat it with care, and welcome it there with love
It may be I, so do not deny its plea
Crown it with flowers, grant love its hours for me."

> *MARTINE enters dressed in civilian clothes and carrying her*
> *suitcases. She's exhausted.*

MARTINE   Sounds like Ma singing.

ISABELLE   Leave the door open.

MARTINE   *(shaking ISABELLE's hand)* Isabelle!

ISABELLE   Martine!

MARTINE   Too bad we have to see each other again on such a sad occasion. *(She takes ISABELLE into her arms.)*

ISABELLE   It's all right, Martine. You can let go of me. Catherine doesn't want you to hold me too much. She says it's not normal for two women to smooch together.

MARTINE   In the taxi, Monsieur Savard didn't even know.

ISABELLE   You told Monsieur Savard?

MARTINE   Yes.

ISABELLE   You weren't supposed to. He didn't want anyone to know. He wrote it… in his will.

MARTINE   How did he die?

ISABELLE   Dr. Lemieux doesn't know yet. Dr. Lemieux's Catherine's new boyfriend.

MARTINE   Sickness? An accident?… Suicide?

ISABELLE   Catherine doesn't want us to say words like that in this house.

MARTINE   How come Dr. Lemieux was taking care of him? I thought he was in Montreal? Was he visiting here?

ISABELLE   Yeah.

MARTINE   I got on the plane in Stuttgart yesterday afternoon. I couldn't sleep. You know what time it is in Germany right now?

ISABELLE   I can't even keep track of the time here.

MARTINE   Where's he being laid out, at the sacristy or the school?

ISABELLE   He didn't want to be laid out.

MARTINE   Where's Catherine?

ISABELLE   If you'd arrived on time, you would've seen her. You said five o'clock!

MARTINE   I'm a half hour late on a twenty-hour trip! Besides, the bus from Alma to Saint-Ludger isn't the most reliable, and taxis are pretty rare around here.

ISABELLE   Still, it's a drag for the people who are organizing things!

MARTINE   How come Catherine didn't come to meet me at the bus?

ISABELLE   She's taking care of the funeral arrangements for tomorrow.

MARTINE   I'm going to take a bath.

ISABELLE   Martine, did you love Luc?

MARTINE   I know you had a lot of admiration for him. Personally, I always found him a bit strange.

ISABELLE   You could wait till he's six feet under before you shit on him.

MARTINE   Look, you must be old enough to understand that I didn't have to love him, just because he was my brother.

ISABELLE   I'm too dumb to understand things like that.

MARTINE   Let's just say I never considered him essential to my happiness.

ISABELLE   "Essential." What does that mean?

MARTINE   Something necessary, something important…

ISABELLE   "Essential." *(writing the word in her notebook)* This is my note-book for words. I feel like I don't have enough words. I try to use every new word once a day. *(beat)* So how's the war going over there?

MARTINE   *(faint smile)* There's no war where I am.

ISABELLE   They usually send soldiers where there's a war.

MARTINE   Baden-Solingen is a strategic base…

ISABELLE   What does "strategic" mean?

MARTINE   Isabelle, I don't have the strength to explain every word I use.

ISABELLE   You could make an effort. I haven't seen you for four years.

MARTINE   I'm tired. *(beat)* How have you been? Must be lots of guys hanging around you these days?

ISABELLE   Only when I go square dancing. I got other things to take care of before I start thinking about guys.

MARTINE   I don't really like being here. It feels macabre.

ISABELLE   "Macabre?"

MARTINE   It means "pertaining to death," "something sad or grim." Aren't you going to write it in your book?

ISABELLE   It's not a pretty word. I only like joyful words, words that are "grandiose," "splendid," "en-rapturing."

.

The Vic

by Leanna Brodie

Premiered at Theatre Passe Muraille, Toronto,
co-produced with Cahoots Theatre Projects, 2000

Script available from Talonbooks

•

Henley has returned to Canada from her development work in
Aceh to help her estranged sister Tanis. Tanis has fled
a sadistic cult and is sick, exhausted, and scared.

•

HENLEY   Almost. Almost there.

>   *They sit.*

TANIS & HENLEY   HAH.

>   *Beat.*

TANIS   Where's Mom, again?

HENLEY   Church.

>   *Beat. HENLEY laughs.*

TANIS   What?

HENLEY   I was thinking of that time I was getting your coat on for
Sunday school, and you look up at Mom, all serious, and you say:
"Mom, are we prostitutes?"

TANIS   Get out.

HENLEY   ...And she says: "No, Tanis, why would you think a thing like
that?" And you say: "I dunno." So we're halfway to church, and you
look all serious, and you say: "Mom, are we prejudiced?" So now she
gets it, and she says—

TANIS & HENLEY   "No, dear: we're Presbyterians."

> *They laugh.*

TANIS   Look at that tree.

HENLEY   Which one?

TANIS   Poplar, by the swing set. Looks just like the one where you built my treehouse.

HENLEY   You think?

TANIS   Yeah.

> *Beat.*

You know, I used to hate it when you and Dad were fighting—

HENLEY   WE weren't fighting. I just—Sorry. Your treehouse.

TANIS   It meant a lot. Did I ever tell you that? To have someplace I could go. Remember that song you made? "The Treehouse Song"— remember?

> *Beat. HENLEY sings, tentatively, to the tune of "Ontari-ari-ari-o."*

HENLEY   This is a place to stand,
And a place to grow,
A promised land,
For Tanny-O.

TANIS & HENLEY   A place to stand,
A place to grow,
For Tanny-anny-anny-O.

> *They laugh.*

HENLEY   You know, I stole that—

TANIS   I know. I was humming it one day at the farm and Leah said: "Now how would a prairie girl know that?"

> *Beat.*

What? What? What'd I say?

> *Beat.*

Ever since I told Mom about what happened, you've been so moody. Why is that?

HENLEY I'm eating.

TANIS Why are you so mad at me?

HENLEY I just—alright. Goddamnit. Tanny, he—you—your teeth— what is that? Listen: the least you can do in this world—the least—is to look after yourself... so you didn't have the perfect childhood—so you want someone to take care of you—so what? So many people get nothing—nothing—there's few enough of us to keep it all going— we don't need people like you throwing yourselves in front of the ambulance because you can't think of a better way to get a little attention! There: you asked. Egg salad or tuna.

TANIS Well. Thank you for being honest.

> *TANIS puts her head between her knees.*

HENLEY What's wrong? You sick?

TANIS You hate me.

HENLEY Oh, grow up. I don't hate you.

TANIS You despise me. I'm weak. I'm not like you.

HENLEY Oh... oh, come on, that's not—

TANIS —I messed up. I'm stupid.

HENLEY No. No. You're—needy. I mean... you need things... that I don't need. It's hard to remember that.

> *Beat.*

TANIS Why do we do this? I can't.... When did we start doing this? Can we not, right now? I—I need you to be on my side.

HENLEY I am. I promise.

Unless

by Sara Cassidy & Carol Shields

*Premiered at the Canadian Stage Company, Toronto,
co-produced with the Arts Club, 2005*

Script available from Great North Artists Management

•

Forty-four-year-old Reta Winters, a writer and happily married
mother of three, is devastated when her 19-year-old daughter
Norah inexplicably takes up panhandling at the corner of
Bathurst and Bloor, a sign around her neck reading "Goodness."
Reta is determined to understand why Norah went "off the track";
in this flashback scene, she recalls their last conversation, during
Norah's disturbing visit home from university, months earlier.

•

RETA   Is it Ben?

NORAH   Partly.

RETA   You don't love him the way you did?

NORAH   I do. And I don't. Don't enough.

RETA   What do you mean, enough? *(NORAH glances very slightly towards
RETA as if looking for reassurance, comfort.)* Try to explain.

NORAH   I can't love anyone enough.

RETA   Why not?

NORAH   I love the world more. *(She is sobbing.)*

RETA   What do you mean, the world?

NORAH   All of it. Existence.

RETA   *(knowing how ridiculous it sounds)* Do you mean—like mountains and oceans and trees and things?

NORAH   All those things. But other things too.

RETA   Go on.

NORAH   There's literature. And language. Well, you know. And branches of language and dead languages and forgotten dead languages. And Matisse. And Hamlet. It's all so big, and I love all of it.

RETA   But what—?

NORAH   And whole continents. India. Every little trail running off every hidden dirt road branching off from every major trade route. The shrubbery, the footpaths. The little town squares. There must be a million town squares.

RETA   You could spend a year travelling, you know, Norah.

NORAH   And the tides. Think of the tides. They never forget to come and go. The earth tipping in space. Hardly anyone understands them.

RETA   *(suddenly)* You've dropped out of university. You've dropped out of university.

NORAH   I'm thinking about it. About not taking my exams.

RETA   Why?

NORAH   It's just—you know—sort of pointless.

RETA   What about your scholarship?

NORAH   I don't need any money. That's what's so astonishing. I can give up my scholarship.

RETA   Will you talk to your father?

NORAH   God, no.

RETA   *(agitated)* Please, Norah. He went through some—some phases—when he was younger. Way back. Please talk to him.

NORAH   No, I can't.

RETA   Please, Norah.

NORAH   All right.

RETA   You do realize this is serious. You are in a serious psychological state and you need help. It may be some mineral or vitamin deficiency, something as simple as that. Even depression can be treated these days.

NORAH   It's not one big thing. I know that much. It's a lot of little things. I'm trying to get past the little things.

RETA   Norah. The world often seems to be withholding something from us. We all feel that way at times. You have to face up to it—

NORAH   But that's exactly what I want to do. I'm trying to face up to it. But it's too big.

RETA   *(shouting)* You have to talk to your father today. Today.

NORAH   I said all right.

RETA   But you must talk to someone else as well. Someone in the counselling area. Today.

NORAH   It's Sunday.

RETA   We'll go to the hospital. Emergency will be open.

NORAH   It's not an emergency.

RETA   Norah, you need help.

NORAH   I'm trying to find where I fit in. *(clings to RETA and sobs)*

Grace

by Michael Lewis MacLennan

Premiered at Alberta Theatre Projects, Calgary, 1998

Script available from Scirocco Drama

•

"Rood"

Grace charts the lives of six remarkable people in one day, investigating what it means to achieve the grace of meaningful, if fleeting, human connection in the city. In this scene, Paula, who has recently suffered embarrassment in the hands of a lecherous businessman, weaves a story for Lonnie, who has just walked out on her abusive husband.

•

PAULA   "Poet's hands," that's what he said. Thing is, I actually have this, this sort of rash on my hands, and feet? They don't know why. Ugly. When I was a kid, in school? I couldn't help picking at it. They were always bleeding. People made fun of me. Poet's hands. Hope he's right.

   PAULA crawls over the pew to sit next to LONNIE.

So even though he was all weird, I thought, there's something about this guy. 'Cause of what he said about my hands. So I kissed him.

   LONNIE turns to regard PAULA fully.

LONNIE   I thought he was threatening you.

PAULA   He was but I called his bluff.

LONNIE   You're alone with this guy on top of a hill, he propositions you, and then you *kiss* him?

PAULA   What, do you think I'm lying to you?

LONNIE   No, it's just that he could have attacked you.

PAULA   Well he didn't, okay? You shouldn't insinuate I'm lying. I just met you, why would I lie to you.

LONNIE   Right.

PAULA   So I kissed him and then I touched his, his, his face, I touched his face, and boom, he... guess what: he fainted.

LONNIE   Fainted?

PAULA   Yes! True blue human contact was too much. So guess what I did.

LONNIE   You didn't.

PAULA   I did!

LONNIE   What!

PAULA   I gave him mouth-to-mouth.

LONNIE   You gave him mouth-to-mouth?

PAULA   Yes! What else was I supposed to do!

LONNIE   Shh.

> *They look around the church.*

PAULA   I mean *I* didn't know it was only a faint—it looked like he'd stopped breathing. He might've had a heart attack or something. So I'm giving him mouth-to-mouth and actually it's not too bad, you know? And then guess what he did.

LONNIE   He came to.

PAULA   He, he... he CAME.

LONNIE   Shh!—What?!

PAULA   Right in his pants. I'm, you know, resurrecting him—

LONNIE   —Resuscitating him—

PAULA   —Yeah and bam, an orgasm shoots him back to consciousness.

LONNIE   *(weighing the possibility)* I've never heard of this.

PAULA   It's pretty common. I mean, not to me, but I've read about it.

LONNIE   Where.

PAULA   I can't remember. *(beat)* Well in the Bible for one thing, when Jesus brings people back to life.

LONNIE   It doesn't say that.

PAULA   Or when angels touch you: bam, you have an orgasm. What's that word...

LONNIE   That's not in the Bible!

PAULA   ...ECSTASY.

LONNIE   That is utterly different.

PAULA   You think I'm making this UP?

LONNIE   *No,* I didn't say that...

PAULA   I mean, I know it's strange, but sometimes strange things happen. Don't strange things ever happen to you?

LONNIE   Sure.

PAULA   Right.

LONNIE   Then what.

PAULA   Then I left him, ecstatic in the grass, wet spot in his pants.

LONNIE   So you fought back.

> *PAULA scoffs.*

Really, you had the swift, self-assured confidence to, to stand up, hit the guy where it counts. A kiss: his weak spot: exactly what he wanted. Exactly what he was terrified of.

PAULA   *(back-pedalling)* I didn't really do anything.

LONNIE   Sure you did. It's odd, but it's, well, it's very empowered.

PAULA   No, it's not, it's—

LONNIE   You probably touch people like that every day.

PAULA   I don't! I work in the library checking out books, okay? When you're behind a counter most people don't even look at you. I mean, they might watch how fast I can sign out a book, which is really fast, *especially* with them all GAWKING at my ECZEMA. Anyways... I came in here to just... think it over, give thanks. What were you praying for?

LONNIE   (*almost embarrassed*) Well I wasn't "praying"...

PAULA   It's nothing to be ashamed of.

LONNIE   Just trying to sort a few things out.

PAULA   Day off?

LONNIE   Called in sick.

PAULA   What's your job?

LONNIE   I work in radio.

PAULA   I love the radio! I always have it on. So, nobody ever recognizes you, huh?

LONNIE   No.

PAULA   Hey—do you know that woman, the angel of the bridge?

LONNIE   No.

PAULA   Come on, you do, you're just sworn to secrecy, right?

LONNIE   No. Her show will be on another station.

PAULA   I wonder if I know her. They said on the news that she was a janitor.

LONNIE   Bank teller.

PAULA   Right, okay. Hey! What are you doing tonight? I mean, you want to come see me read my poetry? I'm just the, you know, the warm-up act, but it should be really good. You should come.

Gives her a handbill.

I'm on early, so don't be late.

LONNIE   I'll try.

PAULA   See? That's my name there: Paula. I'll dedicate a poem to you.
Um, you know what? You've got this… I can see a… *(Pause. PAULA
finally touches her own cheekbone.)*

> *LONNIE races for her compact.*

Blotch.

> *Her face in the compact, LONNIE performs maintenance.*

Oh. *(Silence. PAULA has messed up again.)* Make-up, eh? Always got to
touch up.

LONNIE   Right.

PAULA   So what happened—

LONNIE   You know, people aren't actually supposed to *talk* in here.

PAULA   Sorry. *(beat)* Well there's nobody else in here. I mean, who could
hear us? *(Silence. They both look toward the altar.)* Whoo. So do you
need a place to stay tonight?

LONNIE   *(slight laugh)* Oh no, I'm fine… I have a place I'm staying.

> *In the next lines LONNIE takes a tube of hand lotion from her purse.*

PAULA   Where?

LONNIE   Well I haven't actually booked it yet.

PAULA   But you've got friends, right?

LONNIE   *(Flustered, she squeezes out too much lotion.)* Damn.

PAULA   Here.

> *PAULA takes some of the lotion with her own hands. The lotion-
> management makes the women laugh.*

Well if you can, come to my reading, okay?

LONNIE   I'll sure try.

> *For a while, their four hands are intertwined in a washing motion,
> applying the lotion on each other. LONNIE becomes fascinated by
> PAULA's hands.*

PAULA   Do you think I'm too plain for someone, like, normal to want to be with?

LONNIE   *(awkward laugh)* You're not plain.

PAULA   Right. I know the first thing you thought when you saw me.

LONNIE   What.

PAULA   Ugly as sin. Fat.

LONNIE   What's the first thing you thought about me.

PAULA   Beautiful.

LONNIE   See how wrong we were?

> *They sit caressing each other's hands. LONNIE looks around the church. PAULA impulsively takes LONNIE's face in her hands. Both are moved by such rare tenderness. With a scabby, greasy hand, PAULA smoothes away the make-up from LONNIE's cheek, revealing the bruise. LONNIE lets her.*

PAULA   Such a beautiful face.

> *LONNIE kisses PAULA, fully.*

Little Sister

by Joan MacLeod

*Premiered at the Berkeley Street Theatre, Toronto,
produced by Theatre Direct, 1994*

Script available from Talonbooks

•

Bella and Tracey are responding to the rumours they have heard
about why their classmate Katie is in the hospital.

•

BELLA and TRACEY in the washroom, a few days later.

TRACEY   Anorexic.

BELLA   No way.

TRACEY   Absolutely. Anorexic. As in Karen Carpenter.

BELLA   Who?

TRACEY   As in Shannen What's-her-name and half of Hollywood for
God's sake.

BELLA   Katie's anorexic? Katie thinks she's fat? That's impossible…

TRACEY   She's nuts. Part of the disease is being totally mental.

BELLA   I wish I had that. I wish I was anorexic just for a week. I mean
I wish I was skinny like that but cured. You know what I mean.

TRACEY   She's at Children's. The fruitcake ward. Correction. The
ultra-lite-slim-fast-fruitcake ward.

BELLA   We should go see her. I've never even been in a hospital
overnight, except when I was born. I didn't really mean that…
about wishing I had it. Anorexia. I wonder how she got it?

TRACEY Maybe Jay gave it to her...

BELLA Oprah had these ladies on, the kind that eat a ton of ice cream and then throw it up.

TRACEY Bulimics.

BELLA I mean they're all totally cured now but this one lady she got to the point that she threw up so much she couldn't do it anymore so she got her husband to kind of grab her from behind and help her.

TRACEY Maybe Jay told Katie he likes his women skinny. He does that. He tries to make people insecure.

BELLA And even the cured ladies on "Oprah", all of them, even though they're happy now, every single one said that every time they look in a mirror they can't see themselves. They can't really see what they look like. They just see all the flaws, all the parts of them they don't like... I do that.

TRACEY Everybody does that. Not liking the way you look is completely normal. The whole world could go on "Oprah" and complain about something. The only people who are thrilled with their appearance at all times are guys. Jay practically has an orgasm every time he walks by a mirror.

BELLA Tracey.... Did you and Jay have sex?

TRACEY Sort of.

BELLA How do you sort of have sex?

TRACEY We didn't have real sex. We just fooled around quite a bit. Correction. He fooled around. He made sure he got what he wanted and then called it a night.

BELLA But it was safe...

TRACEY I invented safe sex. Of course it was safe.

BELLA An you don't think you're too young for sex and all?

TRACEY If this was the Middle Ages we'd both be grandmothers.

BELLA When did they invent mirrors?

TRACEY   I don't know. Probably lady dinosaurs looked at their reflections in the lake and threw a fit about the size of their heads. How should I know?

BELLA   They had tiny heads, dinosaurs. That's why they didn't survive.

TRACEY   If they were survivors they could've gone on "Oprah". Oprah's crazy for survivors.

BELLA   Poor Katie. I hope she'll be okay.

TRACEY   Let's see.

fareWel

by Ian Ross

Premiered at Prairie Theatre Exchange, Winnipeg, 1996

Script available from Scirocco Drama

•

Rachel and Phyllis, two Native women living on a reserve,
are sitting at the table in Phyllis' house. There is a dull
thump against the door. Rachel ignores it.

•

PHYLLIS   *(off)* Do you want some tea?

RACHEL   What?

PHYLLIS   I said, do you want some tea?

RACHEL   Yeah. *(RACHEL puts the outfit down and picks through the butts
in the ashtray.)*

> *The dull thump continues. PHYLLIS comes from offstage and throws
> open the door. PHYLLIS is a larger woman with a strong body. She is
> wearing slacks and a T-shirt. She screams.*

PHYLLIS   You kids stop throwing that ball against the house. Go play at
the dump. *(She shuts the door.)* Damn kids. Did you say you wanted
tea? *(She exits to the kitchen.)*

RACHEL   Yeah. D'you have any smokes?

PHYLLIS   Yeah. In my jacket.

> *RACHEL looks in PHYLLIS' jacket. She searches all the pockets,
> pulling out more and more crap. Tissues, candy bar wrappers,
> matches and finally an empty pack of cigarettes. RACHEL, dejected,
> slumps slightly.*

(off) You should have seen that stupid Nigger at the wake. He was there pretending to try and sing, "Jesus in the Family," but he kept saying it "pamily," like if you're from Dauphin River. And you could just hear him. *(PHYLLIS comes in singing.)* "Jesus in the pamily, happy happy home."

RACHEL   You don't got any.

PHYLLIS   What?

RACHEL   Cigrettes.

PHYLLIS   *(She sits with the tea.)* Those damn kids. That Jamie's stealing my cigrettes again. He's just like his dad that one, never listening to me. *(She notices the dancing outfit.)* See. Look at this I told him to throw this stupid old thing out.

RACHEL   No. Don't. I took that out of the garbage. You should not throw this out, Phyllis.

PHYLLIS   Yes. It's heathen this thing. I just didn't want to say no when Bertha gave it to me.

RACHEL   You disrespect Angus by throwing this out you know?

PHYLLIS   I don't want it.

RACHEL   Well I'll keep it then.

PHYLLIS   If you cared so much about Angus how come you didn't stay at the wake?

RACHEL   I feel bad enough already.

PHYLLIS   About what?

RACHEL   There's never anything good about this place. You notice that? There's always people dying, or waiting to die. I should've just stayed in Winnipeg.

PHYLLIS   Then who would I talk to?

   RACHEL sips her tea.

RACHEL   This tea tastes funny.

PHYLLIS   I don't got any new bags.

RACHEL   Well could you get me some sugar.

PHYLLIS   I don't got none left. I'm trying to cut back.

RACHEL   Why?

PHYLLIS   The nurse at school's been scaring the shit out of me and my kids. She told them they're gonna get sugar di-betes, 'cause that's what happens to Indian kids who eat too much sugar.

RACHEL   Ahhh those doctors and nurses are full of shit. They don't care about us. They come here, feel our heart, pull our teeth and then take off and get their money from the government. They don't give a shit about us.

RACHEL begins picking up different butts and looking at them.

PHYLLIS   I'll help you. You think we have enough for two?

RACHEL   Don't know. Probably.

They begin to take what tobacco they can out of remaining butts.

PHYLLIS   You know Rachel…

RACHEL   Yeah?

PHYLLIS   I'm kinda scared.

There's a loud thump at the door. PHYLLIS jumps. She gets up and throws the door open. She yells.

You kids stop that. Go play at the dump I said. And Jamie you stop stealing my cigrettes, you'll get addicted. Damn kids.

RACHEL   They're just playing.

PHYLLIS   They don't have to use the side of the house like a barn. *(PHYLLIS sits back down.)*

RACHEL   What?

PHYLLIS   Eh?

RACHEL   Forget it. What were you saying?

PHYLLIS   When?

RACHEL   Just now.

PHYLLIS   Oh. Oh yeah. You know Rachel…

RACHEL   Yeah?

PHYLLIS   I'm kinda scared.

RACHEL   How come?

PHYLLIS   I always feel scared when someone dies ,'cause then I know someone else is gonna die too. And with old Angus dying…

RACHEL   Is this that dying in three shit?

PHYLLIS   It's not shit.

RACHEL   Just Angus is dead. That's only one.

PHYLLIS   This time feels like three.

RACHEL   Aehhhh.

PHYLLIS   Sure.

RACHEL   Talk about something else.

PHYLLIS   So'd you hear about Margret?

RACHEL   What's that?

PHYLLIS   She's pregnant.

RACHEL   No way.

PHYLLIS   Sure.

RACHEL   Who told you then?

PHYLLIS   Nigger.

RACHEL   And how does he know?

PHYLLIS   I don't know. Maybe he did it.

RACHEL   As if he could even find it. So Teddy's gonna have another kid. What's that make… four? Ten?

PHYLLIS   That's just what I heard.

> *They now have enough tobacco for two cigarettes. RACHEL sniffs her fingers and then chops her hands together to cleanse then of any loose tobacco. PHYLLIS wipes her hands off on her pants.*

RACHEL   There. D'you got any rolling paper?

PHYLLIS   No. I thought you had some.

RACHEL   Fuck.

PHYLLIS   Maybe we could just burn it and wave the smoke in our mouths.

RACHEL   You can't taste it that way. What the hell good is tobacco if you can't taste it.

PHYLLIS   I don't know.

RACHEL   I don't know.

PHYLLIS   Well don't get mad at me. I don't need rolling papers. I just buy my cigrettes.

RACHEL   Well help me find something. Get some paper.

PHYLLIS exits.

PHYLLIS   *(off)* How 'bout wax paper?

RACHEL   We're not tryin' to make cookies.

PHYLLIS   *(entering)* How 'bout toilet paper?

RACHEL   We need something thin like that. Like rolling paper. I know.

RACHEL exits and returns quickly. She's leafing through a Bible, looking for an acceptable page. PHYLLIS shrieks and immediately grabs the Bible. RACHEL doesn't let go.

PHYLLIS   No. No way. You're not using that.

RACHEL   What's wrong.

PHYLLIS   No way. Not the Bible. It's bad luck.

RACHEL   What? No it isn't.

PHYLLIS   Yes. Yes it is. You can't. This is like a holy book. You can't use it to make cigrettes.

RACHEL   Why?

PHYLLIS   'Cause it's bad. It's bad luck. We'll get in an accident. Or you'll get cancer or something.

RACHEL   It's just a book Phyllis. It's only words.

PHYLLIS   The words of God.

They have a slight tug of war.

RACHEL   Let go. Let go. Phyllis.

PHYLLIS   No. You can't use this.

RACHEL   For fuck's sake Phyllis.

PHYLLIS   You can't use this. *(PHYLLIS wrenches the Bible free.)* We got our names from this Bible.

RACHEL   I don't think there was a Phyllis in the Bible.

There's a loud thumping at the door. PHYLLIS charges to the door.

PHYLLIS   Goddamn you kids…

Perfect Pie

by Judith Thompson

Premiered at Tarragon Theatre, Toronto, 2000

Script available from Playwrights Canada Press

•

When long-estranged friends Patsy and Marie reunite, memories
such as this one from the past come swirling forward.

•

MARIE   If somebody would just tell my why they are doing this to me,
I would be their slave for life if somebody would just tell me what is
WRONG with me. I know I'm not UGLY, aside from my face, I do
really well in school, I'm nice, I mean what the hell is wrong with me?

PATSY   Nothing.

MARIE   Nothing? You promise, nothing?

PATSY   Well, maybe, I don't know.

MARIE   What?

PATSY   Nothing.

MARIE   No, what?

PATSY   Well.

MARIE   Please. Please, Patsy.

PATSY   Well. Maybe... if you had... a...

MARIE   What? *(long pause)*

PATSY   Bath?

MARIE   What?

PATSY   I mean, no offence or anything, and it doesn't bother me at all, but I was just thinking that maybe if you like, took a bath or a shower more.

MARIE   Are you saying... I smell?

PATSY   No. Just a little. Sometimes.

MARIE   I smell? But I wash under my arms with soap every day. I couldn't smell. You're crazy.

PATSY shrugs.

Patsy? *(pause)* Why didn't you tell me this before?

PATSY shrugs.

What... what does it smell like?

PATSY shrugs.

MARIE   Like Linda Perchuk? Not like Linda Perchuk?

PATSY   My mom says that when a girl gets her period—

MARIE   What?

PATSY   That well, when you reach puberty all these strange smells start to happen and well that you need to take a bath once a week.

MARIE   Do you? Take one once a week?

PATSY   My mom makes us.

MARIE   Once a week?

PATSY   Every Saturday night Mom fills up the bath. That takes an hour or two then all five of us take a bath so we'll be nice and clean for church on Sunday. I always go first cause I'm the cleanest.

MARIE slaps herself. PATSY tries to stop her, grabs MARIE in a hold/embrace.

Don't! Marie. Stop that, Marie!... I'm sorry. I shouldn't have...

MARIE   See the thing is... I want to take a bath, right. I wanted to take a bath like every ten days. But the last time I filled the bath my mom gave me a black eye cause we don't have any water see cause we don't hardly have any water in our well, we—Is that Mud Lake? Near those trees?

PATSY   Yeah, that's Mud Lake.

MARIE   We should walk out there one day.

PATSY   No.

MARIE   How come?

PATSY   It's weedy. Brian Ring's cousin from Gan he died in it.

MARIE   Not to swim in it, just to see it.

PATSY   You can't even put a boat in it.

MARIE   Just to see it, Pats. Don't you want to see it?

PATSY   My mother, she grew up here and she's never seen it.

Scenes

2 males

Consecrated Ground

by George Boyd

*Premiered at the Sir James Dunn Theatre, Halifax,
produced by Eastern Front Theatre, 1999*

Script available from Talonbooks

•

A Brief Synopsis by George Boyd.

Consecrated Ground is set in the mid-seventies in Halifax, Nova Scotia.
One of the oldest, Black indigenous communities in Canada,
Africville is set to be demolished by city hall. A social worker
has been dispatched to the scene.

Tom Clancy is young, white and inexperienced (this, his first job!).
In fact, he's been surreptitiously, and cheaply, buying resident's
deeds and issuing Quit Claim Certificates all the while. However,
residents and church officials are adamant the church remain.

In the following scene, we find Clancy negotiating the church's life
on the site. Clancy's motives are commendable, however, he is young
and naïve; blind to the complicated political machinations of city hall.
In other words, Clancy truly believes in the following message he
delivers to Reverend Miner. Sadly, the city is even deceiving him. The
church, along with the rest of the community is simply demolished.

•

> *CLANCY sits alone in the church staring at the pulpit as
> REVEREND MINER comes brushing into the room, removing
> his overcoat.*

REVEREND MINER   Either you're early, or I'm late, boy.

CLANCY   I'm early, sir. Tom Clancy.

REVEREND MINER   Say… we got some coloured Clancys here in Africville—any relation?

CLANCY   No… but, ah…

REVEREND MINER   Cool in here. Maybe I'll start the furnace.

CLANCY   Can it wait, sir? I'm rushed for time.

REVEREND MINER   You're rushed for time?

CLANCY   Yes I have some people to see and—

REVEREND MINER   So you're the one they "sacrificed." *(He chuckles.)* Lord, listen to me. I'm still thinking yesterday's sermon. I mean, you're the one they "picked."

CLANCY   Yes. Is there something wrong?

REVEREND MINER   No, no. It was just I was expecting someone a little older that's all. I thought you sounded young on the phone—but not this young. I mean, you're a kid. Just a boy, really. Relatively speaking.

CLANCY   Relative to what?

REVEREND MINER   Relative to what you're charged to do.

CLANCY   I'm twenty-four, a graduate of Dalhousie University and the Nova Scotia School of Social Work. I have two degrees.

REVEREND MINER   That's mighty impressive. When did you graduate?

CLANCY   Last spring.

REVEREND MINER   Oh… master of the world!

CLANCY   Sir, I—

REVEREND MINER   Call me "Reverend" like everybody else.

CLANCY   Life experience wasn't a prerequisite when the city posted this job. I simply applied. I got the job and you're the first one to mention—

REVEREND MINER   I see. Well, "boy"—I'm sorry—"Mister Clancy."

CLANCY   Call me what you want, Reverend. I've been called everything since I got on-site: "Sonny," "kid," "little boy," "man"—everything since I got on the site.

REVEREND MINER   Boy—and don'tcha forget this—this job is gonna require a lot of life experience from you. A lot of soul searching and not a little grief. I mean, what are they doing down there thrusting a job like this on a kid?

CLANCY   I guess you'll have to ask them. Anyway, as I mentioned, I'm really strapped for time, Reverend. Can we get down to business?

REVEREND MINER   By all means.

CLANCY opens his attaché case.

CLANCY   Here's your envelope, sir, hand delivered. It's the agenda for the Mayor's Africville Committee meeting.

REVEREND MINER   I see. Our friends at city hall are very efficient—aren't they?

He opens it and pauses.

CLANCY   The committee will meet twice a month.

REVEREND MINER   Yes, I already know.

CLANCY   Sir?

REVEREND MINER   I know you have an agenda and you probably have your speech ready. So let's not beat around the bush and get down to brass tacks. There's nothing you can tell me on behalf of the city that I haven't already discussed with the city. Nothing you can tell me that I already don't know about.

CLANCY   Reverend?

REVEREND MINER   It rather seems that the city was of the opinion that the performance of your duties left something to be desired. And at a little meeting they asked me to attend, they thought your presence wasn't particularly needed. It was agreed that I would help you bring your task to a swift and successful conclusion.

CLANCY   (*nervously*) Yes, well… yes, ah, that was brought to my attention—the need for expediency and all—and well, as you apparently already know, unless we can get everyone to agree to our offer, the city is prepared to expropriate this land. That's not public knowledge yet, but we don't have much time. With your help, I believe we can convince everyone to sell and avoid expropriation.

There's a long pause.

Reverend?

REVEREND MINER   Do you really know—do you really understand— what you're getting yourself into?

CLANCY loudly snaps the attaché case shut.

CLANCY   It's not often a kid my age gets an opportunity like this, Reverend. I mean, I can write a book, maybe a master's thesis. Build a career based on what happens on this site.

REVEREND MINER   Good, because Africville is more than anyone's "site." It's more than a headline or a paper for a master's thesis; a so-called "career-builder." It's a way of life. Now you keep asking me to keep quiet. Well I'm asking you about my concerns for the church.

CLANCY   The church stays, Reverend. That's done, but without our agreement we'll have a circus on our hands.

REVEREND MINER   No "we" won't. You boy, you and the city will have a circus on your hands. I mean what's the problem here—the real problem here? *(beat)* They say they can't provide water and basic amenities to the people here? Well in the years to come—and you mark my words—when they build a park or a shipping terminal or whatever they decide to build here—just see if those establishments don't have paved roads, sewage and running water, okay? Just observe... observe... and mark my words.

CLANCY   Are you saying the city's lying, Reverend Miner?

REVEREND MINER   I'm saying they're not telling all the truth. I'll tell the whole truth... at the appropriate time.

CLANCY   All I want, Reverend, is a full and fair hearing, that's all. I mean before the onslaught of opinions and editorials and—

REVEREND MINER   Just because I listen to the city's plans, doesn't mean I condone them. I realize the inevitable—

CLANCY   All I'm asking for is a chance. I can make this a smooth transition.

REVEREND MINER   For who? A smooth transition for who? You and the city?

> *A long pause.*

All I need to know is does the church stay?

CLANCY   It does. That's correct.

REVEREND MINER   Then good-day to you sir. I've got to get some warmth in God's house.

> *REVEREND MINER exits.*

Respectable

by Ron Chambers

Premiered at Alberta Theatre Projects, Calgary, 2001

Script available from Playwrights Guild of Canada

•

Saul and Hork debate taking a job that may be a little on the shady side.

•

Lights up. SAUL, HORK. Coffees.

SAUL   This guy. He's a businessman.

HORK   He is?

SAUL   Oh yeah. Member of the business community. Chamber of Commerce. He's a Knight of Columbus, an Optimist. In them businessman clubs. He's an oddfellow.

HORK   Christ. He's up there.

SAUL   Oh yeah. He's a Mason all right. Has a pretty legitimate idea he wants us to work on with him. A great idea. Needs us for it.

HORK   Wants us.

SAUL   Gotta have us.

HORK   Oh yeah!

SAUL   Oh yeah!

Pause.

So…

HORK   I got this scab, though.

SAUL   Scab? What? Aa?

HORK   Got this scab. Can't work right now.

SAUL   Scab? You have a… scab? Can't—listen… he's cool—can't get rid of a scab? Super guy! It'll go away—he is a really—a *scab*?… wait you talk to him… what's the big thing…. Thinks like a… like a… like a…. A scab… great fellow—scab gets rid of itself.

HORK   No, it's a reappearing scab.

SAUL   Aaa?

HORK   Back of my neck—under my hair. See?

SAUL   That's a hell of a scab.

HORK   I turn my neck. See? Cracks, eh? Bleeds gets all pussed up. Jesus! Takes a scab like that to piss a guy off, eh?

SAUL   Christ.

HORK   Can't do a job. Got to hold my neck straight. Finish this scab off once and for all. Al's gonna put me up, lend me some money.

SAUL   That's a hell of a scab.

HORK   Gives me headaches, this Christly thing.

SAUL   Christ.

HORK   Ugly! Like walking around with this… this… walking around with a cold pizza on your neck.

SAUL   That's a hell of a scab.

HORK   Ties. No way. Not a tie man, but ya know.

SAUL   Gotta get rid of it. No question. But Hork, listen, aa? Can you hold on? I… this is a hell of a job. Job to kiss ass for, this one. Know you don't like to kiss ass, but I'd kiss anybody's butt for this one. Spectacular opportunity for a couple of fellows of our magnitude. You know? Aa? Well. You… what it is I'm getting at here is: Hork—If you could let that scab bleed another week or so—You know, until we get *into* this… Hork, I can tell you: I am certain—if you can put that scab out of your mind till we get rolling—well—there is profit available. Profitability. Us. You know. Let it bleed. Aaa?

HORK   Saul. I mean…. It's profuse. Cracks, bleeds, runs down my arm. Feel faint. Loss of blood.

SAUL   How'd you get it?

HORK   Sunburn. Party. Pissed. Outside. Some… some… woman… this… big boobied…, this… creamy-eyed… all I can remember… sorceress gave me some pills. Mexican sleeping pills. Or something. Something Mexican. Some Mexican shit. Great shit, she says. Mexican, she says.

SAUL   You wasn't thinking you was just looking at them titties and popped a couple, aa?

HORK   For fifteen minutes, could'a ran my dick through a meat grinder: would'a giggled at the sight. Then: black. Woke up. On my stomach. Don't remember a thing. Somebody took my wallet. And my COMB. Some bastard stole my comb! I had that comb eleven years! Hot sunny day. Lay there maybe two days, I don't know. One anyway. But. Wind blew my hair up. I'm usually conscious of the ultraviolet radiation's potential to cause dermatological damage. Had all my clothes on. But the prick wind blew my hair up and exposed my neck! Got scorched. Fuck!

SAUL   Put a bandage on it.

HORK   It's gotta be at the air!

SAUL   Okay!

HORK   So it dries out!

SAUL   OKAY look Hork!

HORK   CHRIST!

SAUL   OKAY! Look… don't want to get nasty, now, you know, but it's like this I guess, aaa, it's the SCAB or the JOB. Aaaa? The SCAB or the JOB. Pick one! Okay! Just pick one! Just let me know now, I'll get off your ass.

HORK   Okay!

SAUL   Okay!

HORK   Okay!

SAUL   You've picked?

HORK   I picked.

SAUL   Pick the right one? Aa? Should I go on? Aa?

HORK   Yeah. You ought to go on. Okay.

SAUL   OKAY. So... he's gonna engineer the whole thing.

HORK   Engineer? So what is this? Is this a scam? Is this illegal? Cause, why would a legitimate businessman hire... hire us? Huh? Coupla... coupla... whatever we are.... Is this something greasy?

SAUL   I asked him same thing. Same thing. "Is this something greasy?" I ask. "I'm a legitimate businessman," he says. "Absolutely," I say. "I said it," he says, "so I am." "I asked cause I was curious," I say. "Sign of an active mind," he says. "Don't do anything greasy," I say. "This isn't greasy," he says, "I'm an Odd Fellow." "That's what I hear," I say. "I speak the truth," he says. "That's good," I say, "Cause greasy stuff is out for me." "It's not greasy in the least," he says.

HORK   So what is it?

SAUL   Well, it's fireworks.

HORK   What?

SAUL   It's a fireworks job.

HORK   Fireworks. What d'ya mean fireworks?

SAUL   FIREWORKS!! You know. Gas station fireworks. You know. You got a kid. You pull into a gas station, they got a big sign: FIREWORKS, "Daddy! Daddy! Buy me some fucking fireworks. Please! Please! Can I have some fucking fireworks, Daddy?" So you buy the kid one of them backyard fireworks. You know, like a snow cone or whatever...

HORK   A roman candle.

SAUL   Is that one?

HORK   Firecrackers.

SAUL   Yeah!

HORK   Then they got them small ones, them ladyfingers ones.

SAUL   That's it!

HORK   Fireworks, eh?

SAUL   Fireworks, buddy!

HORK   You pay ten bucks for one of these things pull up the lawn chairs and light it like it's going to be the greatest spectacle you ever saw and it fizzles on for two minutes and it's over.

SAUL   Fireworks! Good clean fun! Something like this, something like this I can get behind. None of that Many Level Marketing beauty cream shit. None of that selling useless shit door to door no more. None of that phone sex 900 number shit we tried to get into. That stuff is criminal. No: Fireworks. Clean, family fun.

HORK   I'd buy him a pizza instead.

SAUL   Huh? Aaa? A pizza?

HORK   Absolutely. At least with a pizza you're... you're getting nourished. Eh? Talking to the kid while you're eating the pizza. "Hey, my son. How's your pepperoni pizza?" "It's good, Pop." That shit, eh?

SAUL   It's the same thing.

HORK   It's not the same thing! Why is it the same thing?

SAUL   You eat a pizza you just shit it out later. Same thing.

HORK   Yeah, but at least you're getting something out of it. Christ you're a dickhead.

SAUL   Food, fireworks: same category.

HORK   So what is this work?

SAUL   We have to distribute the stuff.

HORK   Uh huh. Like shipping and receiving. Boxes. Huh?

SAUL   Buys his fireworks in large quantities. Big huge quantities. But he only brings them in a bit at a time. Small quantities. So... what the hell... how can I—I want to—you see how this won't bother the scab—I need to explain—he—see—he's got a big pile of—not a pile—an order… he's got this… Christ, I'm spilling my coffee—he's got—out on the coast—you know… some… it's all… most of it is *stored* there. Okay. And he brings it here. In small quantities. But… how do I… it's mathematical… he brings them across regularly… so… there's more here… eventually than there is… than there—like than there was there. *Fuck.* Okay. But where are you going to store these things before you wholesale them. Aa? Okay I really understand this part. Aa? He's got truckloads of fireworks piling up here. Gunpowder. Aaa? Truckloads of gunpowder. He needs a goddamn bunker to put them in, aa? You know what a bunker is? Aa? Okay. Let me put it this way: Some fire chief would eat his fucking hose if he found all that gunpowder stored in one place.

HORK   So this ain't legal?

SAUL   It's FIREWORKS. It's kid's stuff! As long as we keep moving the stuff. You know. As long as it's…. As long as it's… you know… on the road. Aaa? Get it?

HORK   Sounds like it's not legal. You said it was legal.

SAUL   It is! We do the warehouse we do the route we go home we get drunk we get laid whatever.

HORK   Big territory?

SAUL   Two hundred miles in every direction, Hork.

HORK   Yeah. And what do we get paid for this?

SAUL   Commission. Eight, ten, twelve per cent… I dunno… two…. He told me I don't remember it's a hell of a lot. Aaa?

HORK   I don't know. I don't want to get in some shitty illegal thing and then get caught and go back to jail. I don't want to do that. I want to live legal.

SAUL   Oh you don't know what the fuck you want!

HORK   I do! I just got to make a bit of money. That's all. Enough to get cleaned up. Eh?

SAUL   IT IS LEGAL. You just have to be careful so no one knows about it.

HORK   Maybe get myself an old camper for the truck. And I'll just drive around, camp, get tail. Do a job for a while here or there just long enough to buy a couple of months worth of gas and groceries. And I'll spend the rest of the time out on an adventure. Eh? Maybe I'll even find some permanent puss to have along with me.

SAUL   It's LEGAL!!

HORK   That would be real nice. That would tame me, I'll tell you. Permanent puss. I'll have to think about that.

SAUL   Let's meet the guy.

HORK   Don't feel good. My scab…

SAUL   Piss on your scab! We're meeting the guy! We're meeting him tomorrow. I got it set up.

HORK   You got it set up?

SAUL   I got it set up.

cherry docs

by David Gow

Premiered at Factory Theatre, Toronto,
co-produced with Volcano, 1998

Script available from Scirocco Drama

•

cherry docs is about a neo-Nazi Skinhead (Mike)
on trial for a racially motivated murder, who is rigorously
defended by a Jewish liberal legal aid lawyer (Danny).

•

DANNY and MIKE meet, interview room, jail.

DANNY   How many legal aid lawyers have you met with?

MIKE   What do you mean? *(pause)* None.

DANNY   How many before me?

MIKE   In my life?

DANNY   I am going to indulge in a little colloquial language for
a moment here. *(pause)* Don't get fucking smart with me. *(MIKE
is taken aback by this.)* That's a little personal commentary, do you
understand?

MIKE   Uh huh.

DANNY   No?

MIKE   No.

DANNY   No way am I doing this.

MIKE   What did I do?

DANNY I don't want to hear 'uh huh' from you. The Court is not going to like 'uh huh.'

MIKE What would you like to hear?

DANNY I'd like to hear you say, "I understand that you were making a little off-the-record, personal commentary."

MIKE I understand that you were making a little off-the-record, personal commentary.

DANNY Mr. Dunkelman.

MIKE Mr. Dunkelman, sir.

DANNY Are you being smart?

MIKE No, sir.

DANNY Don't call me sir.

MIKE Right.

DANNY Do you know what kind of name Dunkelman is?

MIKE I know it's not Irish.

DANNY Exactly. It's not Irish, not in the least. It is a Jewish name. Which makes me…?

MIKE A person with a Jewish name…?

DANNY Right.

MIKE You're a Jew?

DANNY Is that what I said?

MIKE So you're not?

DANNY What difference does it make to you?

MIKE I'd like to know where I stand.

DANNY If they sent you a legal aid lawyer who's Jewish how would you feel about that?

MIKE Works fine for me. Works great when you think about it. Are you any good?

DANNY   No, I failed. I failed everything. My entrance exams, the bars, that's why I'm working as a lawyer. I'm totally incompetent.

MIKE   I like your sense of humour.

DANNY   That's great.

MIKE   Oh. *(pause)* Well, I don't mind that you're Jewish if that's what you're wondering about.

DANNY   Thank you, thank you so much. I'll wire my parents. Better, I'll wire Moses. "Moses tell God they're lightening up down here." You are a little prick aren't you?

MIKE   So, your parents are Jewish?

DANNY   Fuck you, sport.

MIKE   You're very angry.

DANNY   I don't like Skinheads. I don't like neo-Nazis, and I'm not fond of tattoos. *(pause)* I think the crime you're charged with is… ugly. *(pause)* So I'm not much inclined to like you. You can ask for someone else to be assigned, I think…

MIKE   You don't have to like me, I'm not asking anyone to like me.

DANNY   *(pause)* That's refreshing.

MIKE   For your knowledge (for the record), I did the crime. For the record, I was heavily intoxicated.

> *The straightforwardness of this makes a minor impression on DANNY. A pause.*

DANNY   …You say you were intoxicated? Did the police test your blood?

MIKE   No. But I think it was pretty obvious when they picked me up.

DANNY   What did you drink?

MIKE   A fifth of Scotch and three or four pints of Rickard's Red.

DANNY   So you were quite inebriated?

MIKE   I was pissed out of my skull.

DANNY   Anything else?

MIKE A little pot.

DANNY Where did the drinking take place?

MIKE At a concert.

DANNY Which was…?

MIKE By a band called HURC.

DANNY Is that something to do with Hercules?

MIKE No.

DANNY What kind of name is HURC?

MIKE It stands for Holy Useful Racial Cleansing. *(short pause)* It's a pun.

DANNY *(nodding)* Yeah, I got that. *(Looks down and writes for a moment. He then looks at a file.)* It says here you were wearing steel-toed, cherry Doc Martens combat boots, is that right?

MIKE Yeah, cherry docs. Eighteen holes.

DANNY It also alleges you kicked the victim thirty-odd times while wearing those boots, is that right?

MIKE Yes, sir.

DANNY Don't call me sir. *(pause)* Why were you wearing those *particular* boots?

MIKE Steel toes? It's part of the recognizable uniform, Mr. Dunkelman.

DANNY Do me a favour. Just don't say my name… okay?

MIKE Okay.

DANNY *(handing MIKE a folder)* Would you mind reading this to me?

MIKE *(reads)* "The victim suffered heavy internal haemorrhaging, and structural damage to the spine, which would have made walking again difficult at best. As well, he had what is referred to as an intellectual impairment, more specifically he was having trouble speaking. The attack is characterized as prolonged, the examining physicians feel it must have lasted two to three minutes." Which is kind of long when you think of it. "He lost sight in one eye as well. He died three weeks after the incident, from related brain trauma."

DANNY   *(A pause, MIKE gives DANNY back the file.)* Anyway, Mike, what I'd like to know, to get an idea of how you might present in trial is, how do you feel about this?

MIKE   Can I say something to you?

DANNY   Sure. Are you going to answer my question?

MIKE   Yeah, I will. I just wanted to say you don't look like a Jew.

DANNY   Mnnhmnn. Neither do you. You don't look like a Jew.

Blueprints from Space
by Mark Leiren-Young

Premiered at the Citadel Theatre, Edmonton 1991

Script available from Playwrights Guild of Canada

•

"Anomalies"

Mike and Tyler have been best friends forever—and Mike has always been willing to buy into Tyler's wild ideas. Until now.

•

TYLER KIRBY is tinkering on a car... his friend MIKE is watching.

TYLER   Almost done.

MIKE   It's been almost done since we were kids.

TYLER   Almost done for today, anyway.

MIKE   You should design things, you know. For real companies. None of this home handyman, Mister Fix-it crap. You're too good for that. You really are, man.

TYLER   All I do is put stuff back together.

MIKE   That's bullshit.... When you fixed up your Dad's pick-up it rode faster and smoother than it did when it rolled out of the shop. And you know it. People take stuff to you that ain't even broken because they know you'll make it better than it was.

TYLER   And just who do you expect is going to hire me? When's the last time Chevrolet ran an ad looking for grade ten drop-outs to design their next line of Camaros?

MIKE   Is that all you're worried about? When you're real good you don't always need a piece of paper to say it.

TYLER   So you really think I could be like a professional designer?

MIKE   Any day.

TYLER   So what am I supposed to design—new cars, a better mousetrap?

MIKE   Maybe better cars and a new mousetrap. You can design whatever you want.

TYLER   You really think so?

MIKE   Sure. Why? What are you up to?

TYLER   Nothin', just thinking. That's all…. You ever seen a UFO?

MIKE   You mean like the kind that kidnapped Elvis?

TYLER   Yeah.

MIKE   No. Don't think so.

TYLER   Do you believe in stuff like that?

MIKE   Anything's possible.

TYLER   Do you think I could design one?

MIKE   What? A flying saucer. You're kidding, right? You're not kidding.

TYLER   I built the bi-plane.

MIKE   Hell that thing was great. It was like the type of thing they advertise at the back of old comic books—build a World War One fighter plane in your own backyard. Kit and complete instructions only twelve ninety-nine.

TYLER   Plus tax.

MIKE   Right, plus tax.

TYLER   So what do you think?

MIKE   Sure you could build a flying saucer if you wanted to. I'm sure you could build a time machine and a Star Trek transporter beam if you wanted. That's why I think—

TYLER   That I should move to the mainland. Work for some greasy boss at a huge corporation where nobody knows your name. Bust my butt for twenty years so that one day, if I'm lucky, I can make enough money to afford to move to a nice quiet place like this and tinker in my shop.

MIKE   Something like that.

TYLER   Real tempting.

MIKE   You oughta give real life a shot. It's really not that bad.

TYLER   Maybe someday.

MIKE   You're mother isn't going to die, Tyler. Ever. I'm absolutely convinced of it. I don't care how much trouble she says her arthritis is giving her. Maybe if the bomb drops or the earthquake finally comes and a big tidal wave hits and the whole island goes glub glub and makes like Atlantis, but other than that she is not gonna die so if that's what you're waiting for…

TYLER   That is not what I'm waiting for. There's stuff to do here.

MIKE   Like what, building flying saucers.

TYLER   What's eating you? You want me to shut up about leaving? I'll shut up.

TYLER   It's okay.

MIKE   Seriously.

TYLER   I'm fine.

MIKE   Then what's this bullshit about flying saucers?

TYLER   It's not bullshit. I've got this idea in my head.

MIKE   Uh oh. What kind of idea?

TYLER   An idea idea. I can't explain it. It's just something in my head.

MIKE   You mean like the fighter plane?

TYLER   Sort of. *(beat)* If there's something out there, if they really do have flying saucers right, then those things have gotta be amazing. They move like, well, like dreams. You know how when you're in a dream and one second you're walking in the desert and the next second you're on a fishing boat in the ocean? That's how fast these things move. Now if I could figure out how something could move that fast.

MIKE I think NASA would have that one figured out by now, man. I mean, the best scientific minds in the world can only make things go as fast as the speed of light or something like that.

TYLER Maybe. But what if they're looking in the wrong place? All these people are following the same rules, right? They're all working from the same book. But I don't have that book. I've just got this idea in my head and it's like a blueprint. And it's not like the books that they use at NASA. It's something new.

MIKE So you've got this idea in your head, this blueprint, for a flying saucer?

TYLER Yeah.

MIKE So it's like a new kind of plane?

TYLER Not a plane. Faster than a plane.

MIKE Faster than a speeding bullet. More powerful than a locomotive. Tyler, have you ever—

TYLER Seen a UFO? Oh, yeah, plenty of times. I mean, when you spend as much time staring up at the sky as I do you're bound to see something weird. Just law of averages. Even professional astronomers see stuff they can't explain. Happens all the time. The thing is, they can list off a hundred or so natural causes and practical explanations. Weather balloons, military testing, the Northern Lights taking a stroll south for a weekend. If you know enough facts you can always come up with logical excuses so that things you don't understand don't mess up your theories. It's called (*pause while he looks for the word*) anomalies. Those are things scientists can't explain and don't want to look too closely at just in case it means having to throw out millions of otherwise perfectly good textbooks. Now me, I'm no rocket scientist, right? So I don't know all these perfectly reasonable explanations for stuff that's supposed to be impossible. If I look up in the sky and see something that looks like a shooting star but it's standing still in the sky—absolutely still for maybe five whole minutes—and then the next second it's gone. Like that (*snaps fingers*) I'm gonna say it's a UFO because I don't have any good, logical explanations for it. So, yeah, I've seen plenty of UFOs. Thing is, last night, I heard one.

MIKE   And what did it say? Take me to your leader—we've got Elvis, now give us Springsteen?

TYLER   No, they don't have assholes in space. No words. I saw this thing that looked like a shooting star and then I had this picture in my imagination and I want to try to put it together for real. I'm sure a real astronomer would have a logical explanation for this too, for the picture in my head. It's just your normal, everyday, scientific anomaly. Comes from spending too much time staring up at the sky.

MIKE   Take two Asimov books and call me in the morning.

TYLER   Something like that. But maybe it isn't, right? Just maybe it's real and this picture in my head actually means something. And that would be important, right? That would be more important than almost anything else in the world. If it really did mean something. So what's the worst thing that happens if I try and do this?

MIKE   Men in white jackets bring you a coat that does up at the back, feed you lots of pretty coloured pills and put you in a room with pillows on the walls.

TYLER   The worst thing that happens is it doesn't work. The worst thing that happens is that it doesn't work and I take the thing apart. So there's no reason not to do it, right? If the worst thing that happens is I take the thing apart and build something else then there's no reason not to try and build this machine from the idea in my head. If it does work then I've build the most amazing thing in the world. Maybe even get that job with Chevrolet. If it doesn't, it doesn't. Right?

MIKE   Right. *(to audience)* I didn't know what else to say. I thought the plane was stupid too. But I never said so. When your best friend gets really excited about something—even if it is a little bit crazy—you can't just go up to his happy little balloon and take a pin to it. I couldn't anyway.

TYLER   Thanks, man.

MIKE   Besides, I kinda hoped he was kidding.

Born Ready

by Joseph Jomo Pierre

Premiered at Theatre Passe Muraille, Toronto,
co-produced with Obsidian Theatre Company, 2005

Script available from Playwrights Canada Press

•

"B-side and Blackman"

Two Black males speak on their first experience with weed,
one of which is connected with the discovery of a gun,
which in turn changes how the rest of his life is lived.

•

B-SIDE starts gutting a cigar, continues to turn it into a blunt.

B-SIDE   Where the weed came from. That was Ricky right there. I know
nowadays is ain't nothing big for a 13-year-old to score weed. But
when Ricky pulled that hook up, that was big shit. It was me, Ricky,
two other dudes, inside the stairwell. Ricky was there trying to roll the
shit, actin like he done it before. I know it was the niggas first time,
well first time with weed. Knowing Ricky he probably practiced with
some other shit, so that he could look like a pro. Thinking back, he
came with it, he came with it still. He rolled that shit pretty tight.
There we was, nervous little fucks waiting for him to spark. *(takes
a deep breath)*

BLACKMAN   *(continues with the deep breath)* I'm standing there naked.
My body all shiny. My ass was all smooth like somebody shaved it. My
balls were all smooth. My thighs were all sweaty, sticking to my balls.
And he steps to me, pitchfork, horns, all that shit. But the bastard
wasn't red. He was pitch black, tar black. So he reaches out and grabs
my nuts, and starts pulling. Tugging at my seeds. And like, as he's
tugging I could feel these sharp blades cutting into my sac.

B-SIDE   When that scent hit my nose. We became men. I remember how it just seemed to slide from my nose, down my throat. And that wasn't even my draw. It was Ricky's draw. When my hands were on that joint, all eyes were on me. Niggas were waiting to see if I choke or what. *(smiles)* It came natural, like breathing to me. I took that draw, held that shit in my mouth. Closed my eyes. *(exhales slowly)*

BLACKMAN   *(continues B-SIDE's exhale)* Warm blood flowing down my legs. At first just light drops, but it builds until a heavy thick flow rushes over my skin, and where my scrotum was, now feels like a huge empty hole. As if someone took a spoon and was gutting out a grapefruit. My insides tickled by this warmth coming up my gutted out hole. He grins at me, holding out my bloody crotch for me to see. I think I'm supposed to be in hell. But I wasn't feeling no pain. That was a high. That was some good herb, shit musta been "dro."

B-SIDE   I don't know why we sparked it on our floor. We shoulda known better than that. But true say, we weren't thinking about ramifications. We weren't thinking about getting caught. We was thinking about getting high. Plus we know not to go pass the 14th floor.

Oh fuck! It's like we all let it out at the same time. Oh fuck. Niggas were all dizzy and shit, but we bolted up them stairs like we had all our senses. Musta been 5 flights later, and we standing silent. Ears all tuned in listening to see if we hear anything. Nothing. Whatever sent us blitzing was gone. But we were on the 18th fuckin floor, crack fuckin alley. So Ricky gets the damn idea from heaven that we should open the door and check it out. The two sheep they were all in for it. I wasn't really sure, that didn't seem like a good idea, especially when we was high. All that didn't matter though. Before we could make a move, my eyes caught something, just hanging over a step. I was more excited than scared. I blocked out everyone and just started walking towards it. I picked it up.

Picked it up and put it under my shirt. I picked up food, no more starving. I picked up clothes, no more dressing poor. I picked up hope. I picked up somebody's dashed away burner. Even Ricky's mouth dropped. I beat him to this one. *(motions with his hands)*

   SFX: "Click, click" the sound of pulling back on a gun.

The League of Nathans
by Jason Sherman

*Premiered at Theatre Passe Muraille, Toronto, produced by Orange Dog
Theatre in association with Theatre Passe Muraille, 1992*

Script available from Playwrights Canada Press

.

"One Track Mind"

On his way to a reunion with childhood friends,
Nathan Abramowitz recalls the Zionist fervour of another
member of the long-disbanded "League of Nathans."

.

1979. A café. ABRAMOWITZ and GLASS are 19 years old.

GLASS   I'll tell you what to do: drop everything and go to Israel.

ABRAMOWITZ   Why the hell would I do that?

GLASS   Same reason I did it: find out what it means to be a Jew.

ABRAMOWITZ   You mean you know? Oh tell me, Rabbi Glass: what
does it mean?

GLASS   Fuck off, alright? What do you know about it?

ABRAMOWITZ   Nothing. And I suppose now you lived on a *moshav* for
two months…

GLASS   Two months more than you ever did. And that's not all I did.
I travelled the whole country, okay. I saw things I'd only read about.
Worked the land.

ABRAMOWITZ   Got laid.

GLASS   I did a lot of things.

ABRAMOWITZ Was that when you had your epiphany? "Nathan, a Jew is a-a-a-ahhhhhhh—"

GLASS Go ahead. Laugh.

ABRAMOWITZ Come on.

GLASS It's very convenient to sit here, sit in your cafés…

ABRAMOWITZ Here we go.

GLASS …with your university friends…

ABRAMOWITZ Yeah…

GLASS …and judge, judge what goes on over there.

ABRAMOWITZ Who's judging?

GLASS Come on, Nathan. You sit around, you talk about "the oppression of the Palestinians," the the the "occupation…"

ABRAMOWITZ Yeah?

GLASS All you do is criticize, criticize, criti—you never talk about the achievements.

ABRAMOWITZ Like bombing Beirut back to the middle ages?

GLASS See, that's what I'm talking about. We try to clear the PLO out of Lebanon and—

ABRAMOWITZ This isn't about clearing the PLO out of Lebanon, Glass, it's about innocent people being murdered.

GLASS Don't talk to me about "innocent people," alright? These Arabs, they're terrorists, every one of them.

ABRAMOWITZ You don't believe that.

GLASS Right down to the kids.

ABRAMOWITZ Glass. You're starting to scare me.

GLASS All I'm saying is it's important not to criticize.

ABRAMOWITZ That's exactly the wrong thing to do, Glass. If you really cared about Israel, you would be criticizing.

GLASS   I do care about it. Do you?

ABRAMOWITZ   Y-yes. I mean—I don't know that I've formed an opinion.

GLASS   Well I have. I feel like, I don't know, it's hard to say, it's weird, but: all the things I've been taught, all the things I've overheard, things my parents have said about Israel, about the Jews, the Arabs, the Germans, the Holocaust: things I heard in school, or in *shul*, or on the street— little comments here and there, it's like it's all been floating around in my head for twenty years and now, I don't know, it's like it's starting to settle. It's like a pattern forming, a picture of myself, of who I am. It's right here, inside me, and I'm going to become it. I'm going to wake up one day and I'll be this person.

ABRAMOWITZ   What person is that?

GLASS   Nathan. What if, just for instance, you and me, we split or something, it could never happen, I know—

ABRAMOWITZ   No way it could happen.

GLASS   Alright, as an example.

ABRAMOWITZ   We split up, I don't see you for years, like years, and then one day we get together.

ABRAMOWITZ   Yeah.

GLASS   So what I'm wondering is, would you recognize me?

ABRAMOWITZ   Unless you grew a beard.

GLASS   I'm serious.

ABRAMOWITZ   What do you mean, would I recognize you?

GLASS   I mean: would you be my friend?

ABRAMOWITZ   What kinda question is that?

GLASS   The kind of question I've been thinking about. I used to hate being a Jew, Nathan, do you know that? I didn't understand why I had to be a Jew, why, what connection did I have to it, what was it, it was nothing, it was some backward stupid religion practiced by old men in beards and bubbies waving their hands over the *shabbes* candles. I used to hate knowing that when people looked at me, they were thinking, "There goes a Jew," because in that one word was contained every attitude, every possible response to anything I could do or say. It said, "There goes someone to push around, there goes someone to take advantage of…"

ABRAMOWITZ   I think you're being a little…

GLASS   It's there, Nathan. On my way over here? Three guys passed me on the sidewalk, gave me this look and called me a kike.

ABRAMOWITZ   What?

GLASS   To my face. I mean, this used to be a Jewish neighbourhood. From here to Spadina and all the way down to Queen. And where are the Jews now? In the suburbs.

ABRAMOWITZ   Yeah, because they didn't want to live next door to Italians.

GLASS   The point is: it's there.

ABRAMOWITZ   "It" what?

GLASS   Hatred. Their hatred of us. It is there, and I feel it, and it's never going to go away. And you know where it comes from? From the weak little Jews with their nose in a book, cowering in the corner, letting themselves get pushed around, living behind a wall or blending in with the goy, hoping no one will notice them. And I used to play right into it. But this picture inside me is becoming clear, Nathan. It's becoming clear to me that I'm not a weak person, that I don't have to be weak. Every time I hear somebody say "the Jews are stealing land, the Jews are occupying land, how can the Jews do this" I feel like I want to get a gun. I want to get a gun and get them shut up, get them to shut the fuck up. Nathan I am a Jew.

ABRAMOWITZ   *Gesundheit.*

GLASS   It's all one big joke to you, isn't it?

ABRAMOWITZ   No. More like a series of little ones.

GLASS   What makes you a Jew, Nathan.

ABRAMOWITZ   I don't know. Lots of things.

GLASS   Name one.

ABRAMOWITZ   Uhh—is this a take-home exam?

GLASS   What do you do that says who you are?

ABRAMOWITZ   What do you mean, am I religious?

GLASS   Don't answer the question with a question. Tell me, what makes you a Jew.

ABRAMOWITZ   Oh! I'm lousy at sports.

GLASS   That isn't funny.

ABRAMOWITZ   Fuckin' loosen up.

GLASS   Answer my question.

ABRAMOWITZ   Which one?

GLASS   No matter what, will you be my friend?

ABRAMOWITZ   Of course. Of course, Glassy. No matter what.

The Harps of God

by **Kent Stetson**

Premiered at Rising Tide Theatre, Newfoundland, 1998

Script available from McArthur & Company

•

"Jessop and Mouland"

In the spring of 1914, one hundred and thirty-two Newfoundland
fishermen, selected in fierce competition to join the seal hunt, are set on
the ice forty miles from shore. Captain Abraham Kean, admiral of the
twelve vessel, twelve hundred man fleet issues orders which are
much clearer than the weather; it is deteriorating. "Kill that 'patch
of fat,' then return to your own ship." The SS *Newfoundland* is jammed
tight in treacherous, shifting pack ice, five miles distant. In the first
arc of this classically structured tragedy in three acts for fifteen men,
a storm descends. The men lose their way. In the middle of the first
two nights of plunging temperatures, rain, snow and bitter
blizzard winds, Arthur Mouland, Master Watch, goes in search of
nineteen-year-old Jessop Tippet, who has fled his family group
after his father, Edward, accused him of deserting.

•

*The dark of night. March 31, 1914. Wind. JESSOP, on an isolated
pan, supports a young sealer.*

JESSOP   Henry? Name of God, Henry?

He lowers HENRY DOWDEN's body to the ice.

Is anyone there? *(hunched against the cold)* Someone.
Help! *(gust of wind)* Run. No. Just wait. For what?
Run like the wind and don't stop 'till ye gets...
Where? Anywhere. Henry... Henry?
Damn ye all to hell for a coward Henry Dowden.

*ART MOULAND enters, comes to the edge of the water that
separates him from the pan on which JESSOP scavenges HENRY's
belongings—jersey, sculpting knife, etc.*

MOULAND   Jessop? Who's that?

JESSOP   Henry Dowden.

MOULAND   He was a friend of yours.
Leave the dead lie in peace, b'y.

JESSOP   He was more brother to me than me own two brothers.
Never done a tap 'a harm to no one.
Henry was my friend.
Why poor Henry? Why not me?

MOULAND   There's no answer to that question.
None that will satisfy.
Where's Jones and Bungay?

JESSOP   They're like a pack of hungry wolves.
Or somethin' up out of the grave;
Losin' their minds. Turnin' on each other.
Me and Henry was gettin' far from this cursed rock as we could.
Wine women and songs, b'ys.
Halifax. Montreal. The Boston States.

MOULAND   I had the same notion once.
Turns out everything I needed to know, I learned at home.

JESSOP   I know all I needs to know about Newfoundland.

MOULAND   One night in St. John's town a poor fool went drinkin' wit'
the devil.
Seemed a nice enough fella.
Only the devil had a knife.
The poor fool found himself face down in an alley.
People took one look and passed him by.
A young woman recognized the poor fool—
Someone from back home, he was—
Layin' there moanin' in his own blood and vomit.
She set him up, looked into his eyes; she said his name.
Death hightailed it in the opposite direction.

JESSOP   The fool in the alley was ye.

MOULAND   My Belle tended me wounds and saved me life.
I hates to see another human bein' suffer so.

JESSOP   Who says I'm sufferin'?

MOULAND   Look at ye… pacin' forward and back like a caged animal.
Come back wit' me, Jessop.

JESSOP   Good Saint Art, is it? Ye'll save yer own pelt.

MOULAND   I will. And as many else I can.
My "pelt" don't belong to me alone now;
My Belle is waitin' for me ashore.
She's got the most precious thing on earth growin' in her belly.

JESSOP   Another simpleton born to work his guts out,
To keep some miserable old son of a bitch merchant in the fat.

MOULAND   You got a mind of yer own and yer old man hates ye for it.
Am I right?
Mine drowned himself in fish guts and misery.
Then set about pullin' me under wit' him.
Yes, b'y. Hardhearted fathers. Ungrateful sons…
Long as I was a boy, things was dandy.
My best friend in the whole world, my old man;
'Till I come into me own manhood.
He's dead these fifteen years. I'm terrified of him yet.
I spent half the time angry at meself for bein' afraid.
The other half afraid of me own anger.
P'isoned wit' guilt. And so damn sad.
I got away alright. Then set about creatin' me own misery,
Far worse than any the old brute ever handed out.
On the run, goin' nowhere.
Whorin', brawlin'—the promise of me young manhood
Streeled out behind me in a string of empty bottles.
My so-called friends liked me better drunk than sober.
They was the bars of a cage of me own makin'.
My Belle rattled the door, said,
"You kept it up some nice me son,
But whoever threw ye in here is long gone.

Look at this. They have left the door wide open.
Come out my son. Have a look around."
Well, sir, I did. I seen that lovely woman... my Belle;
The sea washin' through her,
Full 'a tides and currents,
Her heart awash with yearnin';
Mine like foam on the sea...

JESSOP   All the love on earth can't keep a cold man from dyin'.

MOULAND   Can't it? I got the chance to start over.
Nothin' says you won't too.
There's not much left in yer little fire, Jessop.
Join up wit' us.

JESSOP   I'd rather die here by meself then come up against Jones and
Bungay and them.
Or that old bugger... 'tis all the same to me.

MOULAND   Things is orderly back at my gaze; every fella lookin' out for
the other.
I haven't lost a single man, and that's how I intends to keep it.
Come wit' me. Ye'll be taken care of.

JESSOP   Is that a promise?

MOULAND   It is.

JESSOP   What odds? No future here.

> *MOULAND throws his gaff across to JESSOP, who prepares to copy
> from the opposite side of his pan into darkness.*

MOULAND   Are ye determined to die by yeself, in the middle of night in
a blizzard?

JESSOP   No Skipper. That's what I am not.
I got a gaff now.
What more do I need, besides sunrise?

MOULAND   You haven't got a gaff.
Ye've got my gaff.
Jessop! If ye gets back to the *Newfoundland*,
What'll ye say about the men ye left behind?

JESSOP   I'll tell them what I tells you.
I'll tell them me father sent me.

MOULAND   You steal me gaff, ye leave forty men wit' a crippled leader.

JESSOP   Thirty men left me and Henry to die. Fair's fair.

MOULAND   Fair has nothin' to do wit' what ye intend.
It's easy, picking bad over good. Yeself over others.

JESSOP   You got an opinion on everyt'ing, ain't ye?

MOULAND   It's the sum total of a man's choices that makes his life,
Jessop.
You've got a choice, here and now.
No less a choice than evil or good.
I answered yer call for help.
Please. Help me to help my men—

JESSOP   I seen somethin'… somethin' terrible.

MOULAND   What.

JESSOP   Henry. I stood there, talkin' to him.
I seen him… he just slipped away.

MOULAND   'Tis hard to watch a man die;
'Tis far worse to feel yeself slippin' away.
If the devil'd finished me off that night in St. John's town,
I believe I'd 'a come back from the dead and thanked him.

JESSOP   For what?

MOULAND   For ending my misery.
The best life had to offer, stole out from under me, and I'd 'a thanked
him!
Ye mustn't live yer life believin' yer stuck, that things don't change.
They do, my son, for better more often than worse.
I needs that gaff, Jessop b'y.
I'm their leader. They depends on me.

JESSOP   That's where we differs.
I been taught to depend on no one but myself.

JESSOP exits. The fire dies.

MOULAND   Jessop! Jessop!! *(in the darkness)* God help us.

> *Exit MOULAND. The wind rises to a great fury, diminishes, blows a steady gale. Still, silent figures shuffle to life.*

Scenes

various

'da Kink in my hair

by trey anthony

*Premiered at Theatre Passe Muraille, Toronto,
produced by Plaitform Entertainment
in association with Theatre Passe Muraille, 2003*

Script available from Playwrights Canada Press

•

This choral section can be done by any number of
female actors with lines assigned appropriately.

•

LADY ONE   So the brotha said he would call on Tuesday. It's now
Saturday and there's no call. And I want to be cool with this I do.
But it was our third date and I gave it up. You think that was too soon?
But boy when he whispered to me, baby, I like the way you smell. Baby,
the way you feel baby, I even like your toes and baby, your nose. I was
in heaven. And then he grabbed my hair and pulled it ever so softly
and said baby, I like your hair.

LADY TWO   Dark skin brother with a hair complex, only into light skin
womyn. *(two beats)* The naps are showing, I'm perming this. Oh baby
I like your hair? How come no brotha's ever said that to me, oh baby
I like your hair. Maybe it's just too nappy. Too short. It just doesn't
flow. And oh baby I like your skin? Soft brown skin? Not black skin.
Soft beautiful skin. Would he like to feel my skin if it's dark chocolate
and not café au lait?

LADY ONE   So I shouldn't call him? But maybe it's not about me giving
it up. Maybe it's about what I gave up. You know, maybe he thinks my
breasts were too small? Maybe I should have just kept my bra on. That
would have kept these soldiers perky and maybe it's my stomach. He
did grab my stomach and that got me a bit nervous. Too much to hold.

Maybe he's into slim minnie girls. The kinda girls who forget to eat and always order a salad with the dressing on the side. They got issues.

LADY THREE   Maybe the issue is how come you always date dark brothas? How come I always date light skin brothers? What the hell is this on my face! Oh no not a zit I got a date tonight! I'm cancelling!

LADY ONE   I always date dark brothas? Well, they are the ones who come up to me. You know ask me out. I never really thought about it but I just wouldn't give a light skin guy the time of day. They just don't do it for me.

LADY THREE   A brother once said to me, baby, I wouldn't usually give you the time of day, but you're pretty for a dark skin girl. Pretty for a dark skin girl! *(two beats)* What am I going to do with this hair?

LADY FOUR   I want to be bald, sexy and bold. I think womyn are sexy when they are bald. Bald. Sexy and Bold. I'm thinking about shaving my head? I need a break. This shit is getting tired. I think I want to go for the natural bald sexy and bold look.

LADY FIVE   I was once bald. Oh yeah. I told the hairdresser, *(An image in silhouette. A womyn tapping her feet. Two womyn re-enact the following scene:)* Excuse me. I think you're keeping the perm in too long. My head's burning. She said...

LADY SIX   Do you want it to be straight or what? A couple more minutes!

LADY FIVE   So I just sat there. Clock ticking.

ALL THE WOMYN   Tick tock. Tick tock. Tick.

LADY FIVE   Clock ticking. Thinking about all the things I'm going to do with my straight hair. Feeling my hair burn. Clock ticking.

ALL THE WOMYN   Tick tock. Tick tock. Tick.

LADY FIVE   I just sat there. Feeling my hair burn. Clock ticking. Hair burning. Bit my lip. Clock ticking.

ALL THE WOMYN   *(faster)* Tick, tock, tick.

LADY FIVE   Forty-five minutes later all my hair was falling down the sink. I had one tuff of hair just here on the top. One piece. But boy was it straight!

LADY SIX   Well all my sisters have curly hair. Curly like my mom. I wanted curly hair. So what's a sister to do?

ALL TOGETHER   Get a Jheri Curl!

LADY SIX   You ever wash a Jheri Curl and all you had left was a Jheri and no Curl. And remember how you had to sleep with that plastic bag on your head. Your man wants to get romantic with you and you have a plastic bag on your head, because you don't want to grease up the sheets. Jheri Curl juice always dripping on your clothes, getting in your eye.

LADY TWO   I had my hair braided so tight that my eyes hurt. It was so tight that I couldn't sleep. And when it itched I had to pat it. *(all the womyn start patting their heads)* I wonder if Bo Derek had to pat her head. Being that she was the first woman ever to wear braids.

LADY THREE   You ever kept your braids in so long that when you took them out they were dreads?

LADY FOUR   That's happened to me!

LADY ONE   Me too! Three times! Maybe I should just lock my hair so then I wouldn't have to spend four hours taking the braids out, ten more hours to put them back in.

LADY TWO   I'm going to lock my hair. Beautiful long locks. *(two beats)* My mother would kill me! *(two beats)* What am I going to do with my hair?

LADY FIVE   You ever had your hair hot comb and got caught in the rain. I remember I was terrified of getting my hair wet. I would watch the news every morning and if there was any sort of rainstorm I wasn't leaving my house. A light drizzle, summer shower, thunderstorm. I ain't going.

LADY TWO   That's why Black womyn can't swim because we're always scared about getting our hair wet. I remember my mom would say.

ALL TOGETHER   Don't get your hair wet! You think you're White?

LADY FOUR   Did you ever want to be White?

LADY TWO   Not White. Just have White hair. All the things I would do with my White hair. I would have a prince climb up the window using my long blond hair and rescue me from my evil stepmother.

LADY THREE   Cinderella had a stepmother. Not Rapunzel.

LADY TWO   Cinderella had long hair didn't she? So what's the difference. *(She flips her fake hair.)* Oh the things I would do with my long hair.

> *Several womyn come out with towels on their head, flipping it.*

LADY ONE   Well I would just flip it all the time. And just say. Oh my I can't decide. Oh my hair just so long it's in my eye. This hair so long it's in my eye.

Good Mother

by Damien Atkins

Premiered at the Stratford Festival, Ontario, 2001

Script available from Great North Artists Management

•

A woman with a brain injury (Anne) and her homecare nurse (Yvonne) have gone for a walk in the park. They are surprised to run into Anne's daughter Nancy, on her way home from school.

•

The park. Early September. ANNE (forties) and YVONNE (early thirties) are out for their daily walk. It is a beautiful late summer day, busy with smells. They are sitting on a park bench.

YVONNE   What are the names.

ANNE   Grass. Squirrel.

YVONNE   Where?

ANNE points.

Oh that's cool. But they're rabid, you know, and they have mean little eyes.

ANNE   Oh. That's a tree. Wrinkled.

YVONNE   That's a maple. You can tell from the leaves.

ANNE   That's a tree. A big one.

YVONNE   That's an oak. I know that one!

ANNE   That's a tree. That's a baby one.

YVONNE   I don't know that one. Snap a picture and we'll look it up. *(She does.)*

ANNE   Sneakers. There's so many colours today, it hurts my eyes.

YVONNE   I know. It's great. Everyone's outside. Wait. Can you smell that? What's that?

ANNE   I don't know.

YVONNE   It's a spring summer smell.

ANNE   Flowers.

YVONNE   That's ice cream. There must be ice cream somewhere.

ANNE   Hot dogs.

YVONNE   Yep, that too. Are you too hot? Do you want to sit in the shady part?

ANNE   No, I like it hot. I see red when I close my eyes and look up.

YVONNE   Do you? I love Indian summer.

> *They both do it. NANCY wanders on and sees them. ANNE and YVONNE open their eyes.*

ANNE   Nancy!

NANCY   Hi Mom. Hi Yvonne.

YVONNE   Hi. Oh is this the way you come home from college?

NANCY   Mostly.

YVONNE   Cool.

NANCY   I skipped my last course today.

ANNE   You shouldn't do that.

YVONNE   Oh honey, it's not like elementary, nobody's going to give her detention or anything, all the cool college kids skip some classes.

NANCY   What are you doing here.

ANNE   We're going for a walk.

NANCY   Oh.

YVONNE   Did you have a good day?

NANCY   Not particularly.

ANNE   Where's Richard?

NANCY   I told you Mom. We broke up.

ANNE   I'm sorry. *(to YVONNE)* What does that mean?

YVONNE   It means that they don't see each other any more. It sucks, it makes people go wingy. You know someone's been through a breakup if they dye their hair and start working out.

NANCY   It's a private issue, Yvonne.

ANNE   I'm sorry about Richard.

NANCY   There's not much you can do about it.

YVONNE   Sit with us.

> *NANCY sits.*

Isn't it beautiful out, Anne?

ANNE   Yes.

YVONNE   I love it. I love it. I hope I'm tanning.

ANNE   I want you to take me on a walk, Nancy.

NANCY   Yvonne takes you on walks.

ANNE   Oh. *(cries)* I know.

NANCY   What did I do now?

ANNE   *(trying to stop)* Nothing, nothing.

YVONNE   Anne, why don't you go over to that tree over there—the big orange one. I'll take your picture. Kind of far away.

> *ANNE gets up to go over.*

Don't forget to smell the leaves—they smell like fall. Remember?

ANNE   Okay.

> *She is gone. YVONNE has BOO's camera out.*

YVONNE   I think she'd really like for you to take her for a walk.

NANCY   I'm not deaf, Yvonne.

Pause.

YVONNE   Your anger isn't helpful.

NANCY   What.

YVONNE   I know you heard me. You don't talk to her with much kindness in your voice. And if you think nobody notices, then you're wrong. Move over, honey. No—that way. Good. *(aiming to take the picture)*

NANCY   How dare you talk to me like that.

YVONNE   You have a choice here. You can either take it like I meant it, like it'll help, or you can do the usual and get mad, but I think you should realize you don't always have to choose the same response. Anne, honey, LOOK UP, I want to see your face! *(takes the picture)*

NANCY   *(flustered)* I just thought, I mean I know she likes to walk with you, I didn't think she wanted me to go with her—

YVONNE   Come on back, Anne, we need to get going! *(to NANCY)* You think your own mother wouldn't want to spend time with you? She talks about you all the time.

NANCY   She doesn't need me.

YVONNE   That's not really the thing, though, Nancy. You just don't know her anymore, and you don't want to know her. You don't really see her. So you just say, "well shit, she's different, she's not the mother I remember" and it's like you pretend she's dead. She needs you now more than ever, but you're not used to that, you just don't want her to need you.

NANCY   What are you talking about.

YVONNE   It's easier to think that way, then you don't have to put out. You don't have to grow up.

ANNE has returned.

ANNE   What happened?

YVONNE   Nancy and I were just having a little talk, honey.

NANCY   She doesn't need to know—

YVONNE   Why not? Annie knows when something's going on. She's not
an idiot.

ANNE   What happened.

YVONNE   It's not serious, honey.

NANCY   You have NO IDEA what it's like to be me—you just come
in for a few hours every day, you don't have to live inside that
GODDAMN HOUSE all the time—

ANNE   Stop it. STOP IT.

YVONNE   Anne, honey. It's okay. Listen, I'm going to head off and catch
the bus. Nancy's here, so she can take you home. You can have a little
walk. I'll see you tomorrow and at three o'clock we'll see if Dr. Rogano
gets rescued from the mine shaft by the midget.

ANNE   Okay.

> *YVONNE leaves. Pause.*

NANCY   What are you thinking? Are you thinking about the leaves?

> *No answer.*

Mom? What's going on in there? Do you want to talk?

> *Still nothing.*

Mom?

ANNE   I'm afraid of what to say. I'm afraid of you.

> *Pause.*

NANCY   *(deeply stung)* Oh.

> *ANNE breathes deeply, looks away. NANCY does the same.*

girls! girls! girls!
by Greg MacArthur

Premiered at the Montreal Fringe Festival, Montreal, 2000

Script available from Coach House Books

•

"Missy Takes a Tumble"

Splitz deserved to win. Missy stole first place. Set in the cutthroat world of high school gymnastics, this play follows the Friday-night exploits of four fourteen-year-old chums as they seek revenge for a loss on the vaulting horse.

In the following scene, Puss and Jam have encountered Missy celebrating her victory. The pair attempt to lure her back to the woods, where Splitz is waiting to claim the red ribbon, which she feels, is rightfully hers.

•

PUSS and JAM in the park with MISSY. MISSY is pissed to the gills. JAM holds her bottle of booze.

MISSY   It's a party now.
Say hello to my two new pals, world.
Puss and Jam.
Puss and Jam and Missy.
Now there's three names go together better than Jennifer Love Hewitt.
Yeah we're gonna be lifelong pals.
I can see it girls.
It's in the twinkly stars above.
I can see us going through it all together.
High school prom then college days then the job market then how time flies.
I can see us all grown up.

We're sitting in a kitchen with our grandkiddies eating cookies.
We're talking about old times.
The three of us.
Looking back having a laugh.
Yah I love you already.
Give Missy a kiss on the lips.
Let's dance in a circle.
Turn up the tunes.
Blast em.

I FUCKING LOVE THIS SONG.

> *A blast of pop music. MISSY dances madly in a circle. PUSS and JAM smile. The music cuts out suddenly.*

> *MISSY falls on her face, dizzy and drunk. She throws up.*

Uh oh.
I'm down girls.
Missy took a tumble.
Missy's down for the count.
Got puke on her party dress.
Uh oh.

> *Missy looks down at her red ribbon, covered in puke.*

Uh oh.
Uh oh.

> *She starts to sob.*

PUSS   What's with the waterworks, Missy?

MISSY   SORRY MOMMY YOUR MISSY'S ALL MESSED UP RED
RIBBON'S A MESSY MESS
RUN ME A BATH WILL YA?
CLEAN ME UP TUCK ME IN SLEEP TIGHT DON'T WORRY
CAUSE YOUR GOOD GIRL'S COMING HOME SHH SHH.

PUSS   Home?
No no no.
Puss and Jam are just getting going.
Ain't that right, Jam?

JAM   I'm revved up.
I'm a motor car.

MISSY   SORRY SORRY I'M SORRY MUMMY I'M SORRY DADDY
SORRY SORRY SORRY
GOOD GIRL'S ALL MESSED UP.

PUSS   Don't get maudlin pal 'o mine.
The night is a baby.
We got adventures planned.

MISSY   I got a red ribbon.
I'm a champion, ain't I?

JAM   You're tops, Missy.
You're Nadia fucking Comaneci.

MISSY   I'M A CHAMPION SEE MOMMY SEE MY RED RIBBON
MOMMY
MAYBE YOU WANNA PUT THAT ON THE FRIDGE
MAYBE YOU WANNA MAKE ME A SCRAPBOOK.

PUSS   Enough with the mommy and daddy babycakes.
Tonight it's Puss and Jam.
Tonight Puss and Jam are gonna be your tour guides.
And we got a lead on a blowout.
A little surprise soiree in the woods.
It's party boys and party girls swinging from trees.
It's dancing under a full moon.
It's fun and games.
And it's all for Missy.
Everyone's waiting for Missy the champion to make a grand
appearance.

MISSY   Missy wants to go home.

PUSS   What's that?
Did you hear that, Jam?
There was something ugly about that last sentence.

MISSY   Home is what Missy needs.

JAM   Say it's not the end of the line.
Say it's not lights out.
Say it's not that.

MISSY   Missy says it's time to go.
Missy says the party's over.

JAM   That makes Jam sad.
That makes Jam wanna cry.

MISSY   Missy's all messed up.
Missy's party dress is a mess.

JAM   You don't wanna disappoint your new pals do ya?
You don't wanna leave Puss and Jam high and dry do ya?

MISSY   NO NO NO
PUSS AND JAM AND MISSY
LIFE LONG PALS BUT—

PUSS   Then Puss thinks Missy should up and rise to the occasion.
Puss thinks we should fuck off outta this puke park and hightail it to
this backwoods brawl.
What Missy needs is a little adventure.
She doesn't need home.
What's home?
Home is empty.
Home is lonely.
Home is lying in bed trying to sleep when all you wanna do is dance.

MISSY   Missy likes to dance.

PUSS   Then get up and give Missy a kiss on the lips.
Let's cut outta here.

MISSY tries to get up. She can barely move.

MISSY   Um…

PUSS   No problemo.
If vertical isn't working for ya then stick to the ground.
A baby crawl is as good as anything.
And we're in no hurry.

What's it gonna be?
Is Missy gonna crawl hands and knees then?

MISSY   Missy's gonna crawl.
Missy's gonna crawl.

JAM   Then it's settled.
Lead the way, champ.

PUSS   Puss has an idea.
Puss thinks we should play a game.
How bout PUT A HOOD ON THE CRAWLER?
What do you think about that game, Jam?

JAM   Jam likes that game.
That game's good.

PUSS puts her toque over MISSY's head.

MISSY   Missy can't see nothing but dark.

PUSS   *(whispering in MISSY's ear)* Dark is better than having to look at
the shit floating around here.
It's wide-eyed Puss and Jam should be complaining.
We're doing ya a favour pal.
Just wait till we get to the celebration in the woods.
It'll be moonlight and stars.
You'll be bug-eyed.

MISSY   Missy feels sick again.

JAM   Okay, champ.
Have another slug.
That'll settle you.
Now it's off to the races.

*JAM gives MISSY a slug of booze. PUSS gives MISSY a kiss. A blast
of pop music.*

Illegal Entry
by Clem Martini

Premiered at Alberta Theatre Projects, Calgary, 1995

Script available from Playwrights Canada Press

•

"Secret and Private"

This scene takes place in a cluttered garage that these three teens
have illegally entered. Since breaking in, however, they have busted
the opening mechanism, so they find themselves frustrated and
effectively detained in the garage. After arguing what to do
about their situation, Garland, the oldest of the three sits on
a worktable to have a smoke. The other two join him.

•

*They stand a moment, not knowing quite what to do—then
GARLAND retreats to the rear of the garage.*

JIM   What are you doing?

GARLAND   I've got to think. I'm having a smoke break.

JIM   Oh.

STUART   Oh.

*Both STUART and JIM join GARLAND. All three sit on the
worktables.*

JIM   Gimme a light.

*STUART lends JIM his lighter. JIM returns the lighter after lighting
his smoke. STUART lights his smoke, but finds the flame has been
turned up to flame thrower lengths by JIM. He is startled, and JIM
enjoys a quick chuckle at his expense. They all smoke and have
a reflective moment.*

GARLAND   Fuck.

JIM   Yea. No kidding.

> *Pause.*

STUART   Yeah.

> *Another pause. GARLAND retrieves the remote control. He presses the button. Nothing.*

GARLAND   Yea, that sucker's good and dead now. What'd you do before, Stuart?

STUART   I already tried it.

> *Pause. They smoke in silence.*

JIM   You think there's any other, you know…

GARLAND   What?

JIM   Secret compartment kind'a things.

GARLAND   Secret compartment?

JIM   Yea.

GARLAND   What are you talking about? There are no secret compartments here, okay?

JIM   What's that?

GARLAND   That's a *cabinet*.

JIM   Well?

GARLAND   Well what? It's not secret.

JIM   Why not?

GARLAND   It's right there where you can see it. Can you see it?

JIM   Yea.

GARLAND   So how's it secret?

JIM   It's gotta lock on it and everything.

GARLAND   That doesn't make it *secret*.

JIM   You can't tell what's in it.

GARLAND   We don't know what's in it, numbnuts, because we don't know what's in *anything*, because we're ripping the joint off.

JIM   So?

GARLAND   So that's no *secret*, like it's not a *secret*—

JIM   Yea.

GARLAND   *No!* It's like, you don't know what's in someone's house from the street—

JIM   Cause it's secret.

GARLAND   *No!* Cause it's private. There's a difference.

JIM   What difference?

GARLAND   Secret and private.

JIM   I don't get the difference. *(to STUART)* Do you get the difference?

STUART   The guy's not hiding things, he's keeping them safe.

GARLAND   Exactly. Like his wife *knows* there're tools out here, he's just keeping them locked up.

JIM   Suddenly you know this guy's wife?

GARLAND   I'm just saying for instance.

JIM   Has *she* got a key?

GARLAND   I don't know! The point is, he's keeping them locked up.

JIM   Why?

GARLAND   So they won't get stolen and stuff.

JIM   Who's going to steal *tools*?

GARLAND   *We are, asshole!* Jesus, you're making me mental!

JIM   I just don't see the difference between secret and private.

GARLAND   Never mind.

JIM   I mean, if something's private, it's also secret.

GARLAND   Never mind!

JIM   I mean, if you go to whack off for instance—

GARLAND   Aw fuck—

JIM   —that's private, *and* it's also secret.

GARLAND   Aw.

JIM   Well? See?

GARLAND   No that's *private*. That's not *secret*.

JIM   How's that not secret?

GARLAND   Everybody knows you whack off, ya Whackoff. I mean, what do you think we think you're doing in the washroom for half an hour?

JIM   But you don't *know* for sure. That makes it *secret* and *private*.

GARLAND   Fine.

JIM   That's all I'm saying.

GARLAND   Fine! And all I'm saying is that this is a garage, Jim, not a pirate cave, not Ali Baba's den, okay?

JIM   Ali who?

GARLAND   Never mind! The thing is this is a *cabinet*, okay? Not buried treasure. You find 'em anywhere, you find 'em in kitchens, okay?

JIM   Okay.

   Slight pause.

So, you don't think there'd be anything—

GARLAND   No! What do you think?—You knock on the wall three times and a secret box drops out? Feel under the shelf and suddenly—Hey? What the fuck is this?

   GARLAND finds something under the shelf. He pulls it out—it's a small metal box. He opens it. Music plays. It's a music box.

STUART   It's beautiful.

Spain

by Michael Rubenfeld

Premiered at the SummerWorks Festival, Toronto, 2004

Script available from www.originalworksonline.com

•

"The Dinner"

Eric and his girlfriend are working to smooth a troubled time
in their relationship when they invite Eric's best friend Jared over
for what results in a hysterically awkward dinner party for three.

•

*JARED, ERIC and BETH sit around a dinner table. BETH is at the
head and the two men sit across from each other. They are eating
in silence. Uncomfortable silence. The kind of uncomfortable silence
that people work really hard convincing themselves is, in fact,
a comfortable silence. A confident silence. An irrelevant silence.
But it isn't. It's uncomfortable. It's relevant. It's painful.*

JARED   Did we finish the roast?

BETH looks at JARED. He's eaten a lot.

BETH   You were hungry.

JARED   A little.

BETH   There's dessert.

JARED   Great.

Drink. Beat. Drink.

This roast, was…

BETH   Thanks.

JARED   Your recipe?

BETH   My mother's.

> *Beat.*

JARED   Well, tell your mother she's something else.

BETH   I will.

ERIC   She's dead.

JARED   Hmm?

ERIC   Her mother's dead.

> *Beat.*

JARED   Oh.

BETH   It's alright.

JARED   I'm sorry, / I didn't…

BETH   It's no big deal. Happens all the time.

JARED   All the time?

BETH   When you're twenty-eight, people assume that your mother's still alive.

JARED   I'm surprised Eric never told me.

BETH   Yeah, me too.

> *Beat.*

JARED   Well, she lives on in the roast.

> *Beat.*

What?

> *Beat.*

ERIC   She died in a fire.

> *Beat. ERIC says nothing. He drinks a big gulp of water. Beat. There is a desperate need to change topic.*

BETH   So Eric tells me you're editing something?

JARED   Sorta. Yeah.

ERIC   He's having editing block.

JARED   Happens sometimes. Stress. Stuff. Whatever, y'know?

> *Beat.*

BETH   What is it?

JARED   Stress probably.

BETH   No, I mean, the "something." The thing you're editing.

JARED   Oh. This shit documentary.

BETH   Not good?

JARED   It's about shit.

> *Beat.*

BETH   Shit? Like, poo?

JARED   Poo.

> *Beat. BETH looks at ERIC.*

ERIC   Poo.

> *Beat.*

BETH   Wow.

> *Beat. Pause. Drink. Beat.*

JARED   Oh, how was your trip?

BETH   It was really fantastic, thanks for asking.

> *Beat.*

JARED   Eric told me you went to see some art.

BETH   I did.

JARED   See anything good?

BETH   I did.

JARED   Good. Good for you.

Beat.

JARED   I hear the men in Spain are really attractive.

BETH   I wouldn't know.

JARED   Didn't look?

BETH   I've never been to Spain, Jared.

JARED   What? So where were you?

BETH   I was in Italy. *(to ERIC)* Did you tell him I was in *Spain*?

ERIC   I meant Italy.

JARED   No, you were pretty sure—

ERIC   I know you were in Italy.

BETH   What was I doing in Italy?

ERIC   Art.

BETH   I was doing art? So… I was having sex with art?

ERIC   I don't know what you were doing with it.

BETH   You were there when I applied. We talked about why it was important for me to go.

ERIC   I know you took an art course. But I don't know what else you did.

BETH   What does that mean?

ERIC   There are a lot of attractive men in Spain AND Italy.

BETH   There's no Spain. Okay. No Spain. Just Italy, and yes, the men are gorgeous.

ERIC   I know they are.

BETH   How do you know?

ERIC   Jared's been.

BETH   You've been to Italy?

JARED   Spain.

BETH   I wasn't *in* Spain.

ERIC   Yeah, well, at the time, I thought you were.

>   *Beat.*

BETH   Did you tell Eric to fuck me at my art store?

JARED   No.

BETH   Are you lying?

ERIC   Shut up, Jared.

JARED   I told him to eat you out.

ERIC   SHUT UP Jared.

BETH   This! This is the person helping you put things into PERSPECTIVE.

JARED   Have you always been such a bitch?

>   *Beat.*

BETH   You think I'm a bitch?

ERIC   No.

JARED   Sorry.

BETH   Am I bitchy?

ERIC   You're not a bitch.

BETH   *(to JARED)* Is that what you think?

>   *Beat.*

JARED   I think you're scary.

>   *Beat.*

BETH   I think you're scary too.

>   *Beat.*

JARED   Why can't Eric come to me for advice /

BETH   It's about *our* relationship. Ours. Not yours.

ERIC   You're being a bit aggressive.

BETH   Am I making you uncomfortable, Eric?

JARED   You're making us *all* uncomfortable.

BETH   You edit movies about shit!

JARED   At least I HAVE a job.

ERIC   What?

BETH   Nice.

JARED   *(to ERIC)* How can you possibly live like this?

ERIC   Stop!

BETH   Tell him to stop.

JARED   Tell her!

ERIC   This is not what's supposed to happen.

JARED   She started it.

BETH   Yeah, I started it.

ERIC   Yes, you—what?

BETH   I started it. I'm the one. It was me. I'm the BITCH and you're the FAGS. I'M THE BITCH. IT'S ME. I'M THE BITCH GUYS. HEY. HEY LOOK OVER HERE. IT'S ME. BITCH GIRL. I'M HERE TO BITCH YOU ALL THE WAY TO BITCH HELL. *(beat)* AND IT'S A BEAUTIFUL HELL. IT'S THE MOST MAGNIFICENT HELL YOU'VE EVER LAID EYES ON. AND BEING THERE TOGETHER WILL MAKE IT BEAUTIFUL. What was it we took again?

ERIC   Ecstasy.

BETH   I think I feel it.

JARED   I'm high.

ERIC   Me too.

BETH   Wow. *(beat)* Holy Shit.

ERIC   Are you okay?

BETH   I'm *so* okay. *(BETH gets up and stands on her chair.)* Is it okay if I do this?

ERIC   Absolutely.

BETH   I just feel like doing this. Do you guys wanna do this?

JARED   Stand on the chair?

BETH   It's really nice up here.

　　　　Beat.

ERIC   Okay. *(ERIC gets on the chair.)* Get on your chair.

JARED   Why?

ERIC   Because it's *nice.*

　　　　JARED hesitantly gets on the chair.

BETH   Is there wind?

JARED   No.

ERIC   Yes.

　　　　ERIC begins to blow on BETH.

BETH   Oh! Yes. Yes, keep doing that.

ERIC   Blow on her.

JARED   I'm not blowing on her.

BETH   Blow on me Jared. *(beat)* Please please please.

　　　　JARED blows on BETH. The two men stand blowing on her for
　　　　a brief period. It is absurd, sexual and uncomfortable.

JARED   I'm gonna put some music on.

BETH   Oh let me!

JARED   I can do it.

BETH   Please let me do it. Please. It'll be so much fun.

　　　　Before JARED has a chance to protest, BETH hops off her chair and
　　　　makes her way out of the room. The two men stand there in silence.

　　(off) There's so much to choose from!

The men continue standing. Looking at each other. Getting higher and higher with each passing second.

(off) Any preferences?

Music blares. It is blatant Italian dance music. It is loud, and it breaks the men up. ERIC backs away. BETH comes dancing on. The two men are standing in relative stillness. ERIC makes a beeline to BETH and kisses her passionately.

Thank-YOU.

The two start to dance together. JARED watches. He gets off his chair. He is high and confused. He continues to watch them dance, and almost through osmosis, begins to dance as well. Separate from ERIC and BETH who are practically one body, dancing as if it was a mating ritual. JARED continues to get higher. He continues to dance, and eventually, gets lost in the music and himself. The lights fade down to black.

The Pope and Princess Di

by Berni Stapleton

*Premiered at the St. John's Arts and Culture Centre, St. John's,
produced by Artistic Fraud of NL, 2004*

Script available from the playwright at bstapleton@nl.rogers.com

•

"The Other Saint Bernadette"

Bernadette's body is succumbing to breast cancer but her spirit is
captaining a mysterious ship of memory. In this scene she
conjures ghosts of the past to describe how she became a saint
in her own mind. Please note: the Chorus can be anything at all,
one person, a multitude, either entities, or cast members.

•

BERNADETTE   In the beginning, there was me. My name is Bernadette.
I'm named after Saint Bernadette of Lourdes. *And* I've met the Pope.

I'm from Lourdes too! Lourdes in Newfoundland! Imagine. What
a miracle. A second Bernadette from a second Lourdes. Make no
wonder the Pope took time out from his big worldwide PR tour to
come see me.

I know everything about Saint Bernadette the Original, the one from
Lourdes in France. She was really sweet and shy and cute and starved
for attention. So, one day while she was out for a walk, who should
appear in front of her but the Holy Virgin Mary Mother of God!

CHORUS   Aaaahhhhhh.

BERNADETTE   Only Bernadette could see the Virgin. No one else
could, not even if they squinted. The Holy Virgin Mary Mother of
God told Bernadette all kinds of fabulous secrets and showed her
where to dig up a Holy Spring. Bernadette lived out the rest of her

life being extremely popular and very well known and a very successful Saint. So, you can see how the Pope would be anxious to meet me! I was Bernadette! I lived in Lourdes! And although I wasn't yet officially a Saint, I worked very hard all the time to be as Saintly as possible.

Light comes up on GRANNY, behind BERNADETTE.

GRANNY   Bernadette. Stop trying to drown your brother! Get up off his head!

BERNADETTE   Although, sorrowfully, many times my actions were misunderstood. This is not an uncommon frustration for Saints.

GRANNY   Bernadette! Take that rope off your brothers' neck and let him up out of the bathtub! Don't make me have to come over there and give you a smack in the head.

BERNADETTE   It is also not uncommon for a Saint to be smacked in the head.

GRANNY   You're giving me a Royal Pain where my left tit used to be.

BERNADETTE   You just wait till the Pope gets here and I tell Him you smacked me in the head! You'll have to say a million Hail Mary's just to get into Purgatory!

GRANNY   You, my dear, *are* Purgatory!

BERNADETTE   My Lourdes was only a small fishing village hanging off the side of a cliff. I tried and tried many times to dig up a Holy Spring, but there was just no digging through solid rock.

GRANNY   Bernadette. Did you dig up my potato garden again?

BERNADETTE   I couldn't find a Holy Spring, and I never once saw the Holy Virgin Mary Mother of God, not even when I squinted. But I still knew that as soon as the Pope laid eyes on me, He would immediately see that inside of me there beat the heart of a real true Saint.

A drum solo starts.

CHORUS   Pope. Pope. We want the Pope. Pope. Pope. We want the Pope.

A huge spotlight searches the air. Helicopter rotors go thump-thump-thump. A wind howls. A white light descends from on high.

Pope. Pope. We want the Pope. Pope. Pope. We want the Pope! Pope! Pope! Pope! Pope! Pope! Pope! Pope!

Suddenly he is there. The POPE. He is gorgeous. He is loving. He looks a lot like Elvis.

The POPE sings the first four lines from "Heartbreak Hotel."

Cheers and applause from the CHORUS.

POPE   Thank you. Thank you very much. Well looky here. I just clapped my eyes on a real true Saint! It's a miracle! Look at her! Well, there's no doubt in my mind at all little lady. You have got to come to Rome and live in the Vatican with me! You've got to be where people can love you. People here can't possibly appreciate a real true saint like you! You have suffered enough. I can tell just by looking at you. You have got to come with me and live in a state of Graceland!!!!

GRANNY   Oh your Popeship! Don't take her away. I'll double her allowance.

POPE   *You* will have to say a million Hail Mary's just to get *in* to Purgatory, and that isn't counting all of the Hail Mary's you'll have to say to get *out*.

CHORUS   Oooooooohhhhh.

POPE   And, if you are not very very careful, while you are in Purgatory saying your Hail Mary's, I may very well decide that Purgatory does not exist any longer. I might cancel it.

CHORUS   Aaaaaaaaahhhh.

POPE   And then *you* will be null and void. And do take me seriously! I can do it. Remember Limbo? All the little dead babies? Null and Void!

GRANNY   Could I have your autograph? I can sell it down to the flea market.

POPE   Can you have my autograph? Why, I dunno! Is the Pope Catholic?

CHORUS   Ba booomp!

POPE   Why, thank you, thank you very much.

Applause and cheers from the CHORUS.

BERNADETTE   Saints do have to suffer for a while of course. They have to be tortured, mutilated, sometimes boiled in oil, or burned. But God fixes it so they don't feel too much pain. And! There is no such thing as an ugly Saint. Every Saint ever seen in the movies is famous and gorgeous.

GRANNY   You are giving me a Royal Pain where my left tit used to be.

BERNADETTE   Granny never felt anything in a regular way. She only ever had Royal headaches, or, a Royally good day. She often had a Royal pain right where her left tit used to be. Which meant, a pain in her heart. Ever since they cut her breast off, her heart was too close to the surface, and hurt more easily.

GRANNY   And good riddance too! I wish they had cut off the other one while they were at it. Nothing but nuisance. After six kids, my tits were all used up anyway. Not a gig left in them at all. I told that doctor, when they had me on the table, lop the other one off too! Two tits! Two tits for the price of one! But would he listen to me? What do they know? Nothing! That's what they know! Told me the lump was nothing to worry about.

BERNADETTE   Granny. I don't care about your old breasts. I don't want any breasts. Saints can't have breasts!

POPE   Saints don't need breasts. As a matter of fact, you're better off if you don't have any. Mark my words! And now, a teaching Parable. This is a story about poor Saint Agatha. Lovely girl. Came from a good Sicilian family. What a little sweetheart. Happy as a lark. But my dears! Wait til I tell you this! She was being courted by a lecherous Judge who wanted to have his wicked way with her. Nudge nudge, wink wink. When she told him "no," he chopped off her breasts. Martyred her. And the moral of the story is: it's best not to have any breasts at all in the first place.

GRANNY   That's what killed your mother, you know. Should of had her tits lopped off right from the start and she'd be alive today!

BERNADETTE   Granny, you aren't going to say tit in front of the Pope, are you? He's not coming all the way from Rome to hear you say TIT!

Game show music is hummed by the CHORUS.

POPE   Okay folks, now listen up and listen good. I'm going to issue a new Papal Bull.

CHORUS   Mooo!

POPE   Not that kind of Bull! An official Papal Bull! I hereby proclaim this to be the year of the Great Indulgence! How does it work, you might ask?

CHORUS   How?

POPE   Good question. You do a good deed. Or, you give something up. You quit smoking, for example. Or you suffer in silence about something without whining. You offer each little sacrifice up to me and for each one, I will grant you an Indulgence. You save up your Indulgences just like you save up AIR MILES on Air Canada, and before you know it you've got a free ticket for the long trip to heaven. So come on down and rack em up folks!

> *Cheers and applause from the CHORUS. Game show music finishes. "Ave Maria" begins again.*

BERNADETTE   Granny says she indulges me too much.

POPE   That Granny! She's just lucky she caught me on a good day! Now, my child. I want you to take this, in remembrance of me.

> *BERNADETTE kneels solemnly before him. He presents something to her.*

BERNADETTE   It's a teacup.

> *The humming fades out.*

POPE   And remember, whatever you do… stay off of my blue suede shoes!

> *He lifts his robes to reveal his Blue Suede Shoes*

Featuring Loretta

by George F. Walker

Premiered at Factory Theatre, Toronto, 1998

Script available from Talonbooks

•

Lorrie and Sophie discover how different their lives have been,
even though they come from two very different worlds.
Dave arrives, who has just kidnapped one of Lorrie's colleagues.

•

SOPHIE and LORRIE sit on the end of the bed, holding hands.

LORRIE   He was stubborn. He liked doing things I didn't understand.
He liked climbing rocks. He liked going fast in boats and cars. He liked
going by himself to dangerous places and seeing how scared he'd get.
And then seeing how long he could stay even though he was scared.
That's just the way he was. You can't understand it if you're not like
that. You just can't. He knew that was bear country. He knew it had
been a hard winter with not much food for the those bears. He knew
what he was doing was foolishly dangerous. He went anyway. He was
excited about going... I thought about trying to talk him out of it.
But I didn't. I was tired of trying to talk him out of things. It never
worked. He always went anyway. And I was always really angry. And
so was he. Because he thought I was such a fucking nag. So this time
I just smiled and said "Have a blast." And he smiled and said "Yeah
okay" or something.... And then he left. He went off... and got...
eaten by a bear... I mean eaten by a fucking bear. Almost entirely
eaten. Jesus.... And no life insurance. Nothing. Nothing but debts.

SOPHIE   *(crying)* Oh this is so sad.... And horrible. Because your
husband was eaten by bear without knowing you had a baby inside.
Yes?

LORRIE   Yes.

SOPHIE   *(crying harder)* Horrible. Horrible. *(stops crying suddenly)* You know something? I believe I too had relative eaten by a bear.

LORRIE   No way.

SOPHIE   Yes. Long time ago. Hundred years.... Relative goes on expedition into China. Eaten by bear. No not bear really. Panda.

LORRIE   A panda? No way. A panda. Come on.

SOPHIE   Please. You people think panda is toy. Panda eats just bamboo you probably think. Sure panda eats bamboo. Bamboo gone. Panda eats you. Anyway this is a... a... thing we share. Someone eaten. We share that sad feeling...

LORRIE   Ah yeah... I guess.

SOPHIE   No. What am I saying. I lose some relative over one hundred years ago. I have no feeling about this at all. But you lose husband and you have his baby inside. You are sadder than anyone in the world maybe.

LORRIE   It's a bit more complicated than that. I think most people have things happen to them in a certain order in a certain way. But that's never really been true for me. For example. This baby's father isn't my husband. It's another guy. You see, my husband was sleeping with this friend of mine. And I found out. So I went out and slept with a friend of his. And he found out. And then we had a fight. And I left. And then I came back. But we kept fighting. Big stupid ugly fights. And then he went and got eaten by a bear. And then I found out I was pregnant. And then my husband's family found out. And they think it's my husband's kid. But the guy whose kid it is *knows* it's his. And he wants to... I don't know... get involved. And my husband's family wants to get involved. And my mother wants to get involved.... So I left.... And that's why I left. Because everyone wanted to get involved. And it was just such a fucking mess.

SOPHIE   Excuse me. I didn't want to know all this.

LORRIE   I'm sorry. I just—

SOPHIE   People kill themselves when they are knowing things like this. This is too much.

LORRIE   I'm sorry.

SOPHIE   No. I'm sorry. So sorry I might have to kill myself.

LORRIE   Oh my God. Get serious.

SOPHIE   Why do people kill themselves. Wake up one day. A heavy sadness comes down on them. Presses down on the head. Maybe they just say "too much."

LORRIE   But you see—

SOPHIE   This could be it for me. I'm so tired anyway. Who knows. Tomorrow morning I am waking up to the sound of my father yelling like always. Thinking of your baby…. Thinking of scraping shit out of toilets. And goodbye Sophie.

LORRIE   But you see it's not sad. Not really—

SOPHIE   Husband is dead or not.

LORRIE   Okay that's kinda sad. I mean even then I'm still so pissed off at him for sleeping around I haven't really felt the pain of death.

SOPHIE   Tomorrow.

LORRIE   Tomorrow?

SOPHIE   Or day after. Pain always comes. My mother died.

LORRIE   I'm sorry.

SOPHIE   Not today. Before.

LORRIE   Yeah but I'm still… never mind.

SOPHIE   My father yelled her to death. In Russia. He yelled and yelled and my mother died. Then he said "Come on we're leaving this place." He and his brother. My uncle. Also KGB man who has money put away. They are just saying come on. And I am saying but mother just died. But they yell at me very loud very much so I go. I forgot Mother for a long time. Because leaving is difficult enough. But… later the pain comes. I remember Mother. And the pain comes…. Hungry? You can cook in room something.

LORRIE   No I'm okay.

Pause.

SOPHIE   How long you will wait for Dave to tell you what to do.

Pause.

LORRIE   I don't know… I mean these guys. Dave. Michael. I hardly even know them. I don't want them hurting each other but…. You know these guys are like the guys at home. They've all got opinions about what I should do… I mean really that's what every guy in my life has been. Someone who tells me in one way or another… what I should do.

SOPHIE   Yelling at you?

LORRIE   No not yelling… well sometimes. But mostly just… yakking. And giving their opinions like I'm supposed to… listen…. And then… agree or something.

SOPHIE   Yelling is worse! Talking is okay.

LORRIE   I need some time without opinions. Because I just want to *see* how things work out for a while. Before I decide.

SOPHIE   Decide what.

LORRIE   Everything…. Where to go. What to do…. Whether, you know… whether to have this baby. ͵

SOPHIE   Decide to have baby? Baby in there. Baby is coming.

LORRIE   Maybe.

SOPHIE   Oh you mean you will kill the baby.

LORRIE   Kill? It's not…. It's not killing.

The phone rings. LORRIE answers it.

LORRIE   *(into phone)* Hello…. What. Wait. *(to SOPHIE)* It's your father.

SOPHIE   Oh goody.

LORRIE   How'd he know you were here?

SOPHIE   Ex-KGB man. He knows where I am everywhere.

SOPHIE takes the phone. Holds it away. As her father yells. She has a brief conversation in Russian about having to clean the bathroom again. Hangs up.

You hear him yelling?

LORRIE   Yeah.

SOPHIE   Someday he will be yelling so loud…. His brain… *(gestures)*

LORRIE   Explodes?

SOPHIE   Yeah. Or maybe my brain… I have to leave waiting alone now. I'm sorry.

LORRIE   I understand.

SOPHIE   I have to leave… *(She goes to door.)* But… I want to tell you not to kill the baby.

LORRIE   It's not a baby… yet.

SOPHIE   So what is it.

LORRIE   I'm just saying there's time before it's actually a baby.

SOPHIE   So what is it.

LORRIE   Anyway it's my choice, isn't it.

SOPHIE   No it's not a choice. It's a baby.

LORRIE   Fuck.

LORRIE turns away. Goes into bathroom.

SOPHIE   *I'm sorry!*

SOPHIE opens door. DAVE is standing there.

DAVE   Well are you going or not. I can't wait here all night.

LORRIE   *(coming out of the bathroom)* Oh great.

SOPHIE   *(to LORRIE)* I can go?

DAVE   Yes. You can go.

SOPHIE   She says I can go. Not you. *(to LORRIE)* It's okay? I can go?

LORRIE   I'll be fine.

SOPHIE   Okay.

>   *SOPHIE leaves. DAVE comes in.*

DAVE   Who is she? The maid or something?

LORRIE   Her fathers owns the place.

DAVE   So... you tell her what's going on? She looked... like she knew something. Or something.

LORRIE   She saw you Dave. She saw you kidnap Michael.

DAVE   Really.... Is that right.... She did, eh. Okay... so... okay. What do you think I should do about that?

LORRIE   I don't know. Maybe you should kill her. Slit her throat and bury her in a tar pit. I mean, you're leaving quite a trail of evidence here, Dave... Jesus.

>   *The phone rings.*

DAVE   My throat's really dry. I'm having trouble swallowing...

>   *LORRIE answers the phone.*

LORRIE   *(into phone)* Hi...

DAVE   Water.

LORRIE   *(into phone)* Yeah...

DAVE   I need water.

>   *DAVE goes into bathroom.*

LORRIE   *(into phone)* Ah shit.... How'd you get my number, Steve.... My mother gave it to you.... Why would she do that.... Oh that's great.... No she didn't have to know, Steve.... Because who the father of the baby is, is none of her business. At the moment it's only my business.... No I'm not coming home.... No you're not coming here either.... No you're not going to have a say in it.... None.... That's right. None.... None none none!!

>   *She hangs up. DAVE comes out of the bathroom with a glass of water.*

DAVE   Who was that?

LORRIE   What do you want.

DAVE   I... just want to know who that was.

LORRIE   No I mean what the fuck do you want, Dave. Why are you here.

DAVE   You know why I'm here. I told you I was coming.

LORRIE   That's why you're here? Because you told me you'd be here?

DAVE   Well there's this question about my hostage.

The phone rings. LORRIE answers it. Listens.

LORRIE   *(into phone)* Look. Steve. Let's do it this way. You hang up. I'll call you later when you're not so upset. And I'll try my best to explain my point of view. And then maybe you'll understand.... Listen, are you at home.... I'll call you back. Yes Steve I will fucking call you back.... Soon. Later than that. But soon. Goodbye.

She hangs up.

DAVE   Who was that Lorrie. I mean who is Steve. Do I know him. Is he a guy from the restaurant. Is he the manager's son. Or that other guy... the food inspector... I heard something about a baby before. What baby were you talking about.

LORRIE   Dave.... You have to let Michael go. Kidnapping is a serious crime. You could be ruining your life here.

DAVE   Who's Steve.

LORRIE   Where's Michael now.

DAVE   In the trunk. Is... Steven someone from home? Is he your boyfriend back home, Lorrie.

LORRIE   In the trunk of your car? Outside?

DAVE   Yeah.... Do you love Steven. Is Steven the man you're in love with, the man you're devoted to. Is Steve the man you're thinking of when you get that far away look in your eye.

LORRIE   Dave. Go out to your car. Unlock the trunk. Bring Michael in here. We'll all work it out together.

DAVE   Does Steven think you're as special as I think you are. Just ask yourself that Lorrie. Is Steven a man who can elevate you in his estimation as high as I can.

LORRIE   *(shrugs)* Go get Michael. He might be getting really uncomfortable in that trunk. Maybe he's even running out of air. Go get him!... Please...

DAVE   Okay.

LORRIE   Thanks, Dave.

> *The phone rings. They both dive for it. LORRIE gets it. DAVE leaves the room. LORRIE answers the phone.*

(into phone) Hi Jane.... Yes he did. Did Mom tell you she was going to do that.... Did you try to stop her.... She's not "the grandmother".... There is no baby.... He's not anyone's father, she's not anyone's grandmother, and you're not anyone's fucking aunt! Listen, I can't talk now. I'm too mad.

Monologues

female

Real Live Girls

by Damien Atkins

Premiered at Buddies in Bad Times Theatre, Toronto, 2001

Script available from Playwrights Guild of Canada

•

Connie is a quiet, even-tempered woman in her thirties who is driven to the edge by the last of a series of cheating boyfriends.

•

CONNIE   I can't believe I'm going to tell you this. Um. I'm a nice person. In general. Um. Maybe that's the problem. I don't speak up much, um, when I'm upset. I just figure it's my problem, get over it, why bother anyone else, you know? That's just greedy. Maybe I'm just the kind of woman who has "take advantage of me" tattooed to my forehead, I don't know. But I've had three boyfriends in the past six years, and all of them have cheated on me. All of them. What was it about the last one that sent me over the edge? We met in a choir, I mean not professional, well he's professional, he has a band, and he admitted to me that the only reason he joined the choir was to meet "musical" women, which I don't really understand, and I guess I should have taken it as a warning instead of being flattered, which I was. He was always dismissive of my singing, too.

So he calls me to tell me that it's over, that there's someone else. She probably has perfect pitch, I find myself thinking, and then my mind goes blank. I'm quiet on the phone, I'm deathly quiet. And I remember getting my coat, and walking out the door. I hail a cab, and I go over to his place, stopping along the way to pick up a Valu-Pak of twelve pork chops. And I let myself in, because I still have a key, right, and I know he has a gig. I go into his voice mail and change his outgoing message so it says: "Hi. You've reached Jack's Dungeon. For ass play, press 1. For water sports, press 2. If you have low self esteem, and don't mind a man who treats you badly and farts in his sleep, leave a message for Jack after the beep." And then I sneak around the apartment, hiding pork chops in places I know he won't find them right away.

And then I leave the apartment, but leave the door open, right, because it's not the *nicest* building, and I walk over to where his band is playing, and it's raining, and my hair's all wet and stringy and my makeup is running down my face, so I look like Sissy Spacek in "Carrie" right, and I get to the bar and I feel kind of possessed, and I don't care about anything anymore, so I walk right up to the stage, and he doesn't notice me until I'm standing right there, and I stand there staring at him until he says, "Jesus Christ, honey, what are you doing here?" and I grab the mic out of his hand, and this voice comes out of my mouth, saying "Cheater. Cheater *cheater*." And the audience is staring at me with big gaping mouths like I'm gonna pull out a gun and shoot him, but I don't, I just say "Ladies and gentlemen, it may interest you to know the man who fronts this band, the man that you all came to see, this *good for nothing flesh sack of a man*, is nothing more than a dirty fucking *cheater*," and I hear a few people gasp, and I say, "SURELY someone out there has been cheated on," and almost all of the ladies raise their hands, and some of the guys too, and I say "You know what I think? How do I put this? Fuck 'em. FUCK 'EM! NORMALLY I'M A NICE PERSON BUT THE TIME COMES WHEN EVEN A NICE PERSON JUST HAS TO GET MAD, YOU HAVE TO STAND UP FOR YOURSELF, YOU JUST HAVE TO SAY 'FUCK 'EM FUCK 'EM FUCK 'EM. And I'm not perfect, and I make mistakes, but GODDAMN IT, I deserve to be HAPPY, and I am going to LIVE TO SEE THE DAY that I am, AND THIS MAN WILL NEVER KNOW WHAT HE MISSED OUT ON, BECAUSE I'M GOING TO BE SO HAPPY HAPPY HAPPY and anyone who understands what that means, and who's sick of hearing this tired-ass band play, can come with me across the street and I'll buy you a beer using my cheating boyfriend's credit card!" And so we did.

Please believe me when I tell you I am normally a nice person. I'll tell you the funny part though. Well, it's not the funny part, it's the awful part. I still miss him. After all that. You'd think I'd know better. You'd think I'd be satisfied. But I'm not.

Bitter Rose

by Catherine Banks

*Premiered at Women's Theatre and Creativity Centre,
Neptune Studio, Nova Scotia, 2000*

Script available from Playwrights Guild of Canada

•

Rose, 43, has been doing her normal morning errands in her bloodstained
wedding dress. Over top of the bulky dress, Rose buttons up a red silk
blouse and pulls on a pair of red velour exercise pants.

•

CRAZY VAL   Valentine's day—now there's a day fraught with
disappointment. First of all it's in February. The most romantic
day of the year and I've got 15 extra pounds of winter fat on me.
The only thing I can get into are my sweat pants. I wasn't thinking,
"Gee, it's Valentine's Day in six weeks" when I scarfed down that tenth
shortbread cookie on New Year's Eve. So I'm not in top physical form,
which is enough to make me bitter, but then there's the gift thing.

So I get him a gift. I think about it a long time, too, because I want
it to show that I love him. I want to get him passes to the hockey
playoffs or that tool at Canadian Tire that he checks to see if it's on
special every time he buys motor oil. So then, of course, when I serve
him his morning coffee I wish him Happy Valentine's Day to remind
him—because if I don't, and he comes home to a special meal and the
perfect gift, and he hasn't done the thing, he is going to be really pissed
off.

And there is a gift from him. After the kids have gone upstairs for the
night, the beautifully wrapped box comes out. It is so beautifully
wrapped. I take the cover off and of course there it is, the lingerie.

Yes, the black push-up bra, and the thong. Oh God. So let's see, the hockey passes and the lingerie that makes something for him and something for... him.

But that's not the bitter part. The bitter part is that I have to put this stuff on... it's a gift. So I go into the bathroom and I start with the bra. Okay, which is some other woman's size.

ROSE struggles to put it on over all the bulk.

Maybe the sales girl if she is a size 34A. But I figure out if I hold my breath all the way to the bed my nipples might just stay contained in the 1/8th of an inch of lace. As for the thong, the effect is completely lost in the three shortbread rolls that are around my hips. I open the bathroom door a few inches and I tell him to turn out the lights. I ask him, I beg him, please please don't make me come out with the lights on.

So halfway through the dash in the dark he turns on the light, and there is no place for me to hide. No place in the whole room where I can't see the light of lust die in his eyes. But the thing has been started and there's no turning back, and I know I've got 30 minutes of really hard work ahead of me.

But not this year.
I'm ready for tonight.
Things will be different tonight.

Baal

by Rose Cullis

*Premiered at Buddies in Bad Times Theatre, Toronto,
produced by Mercury Theatre, 1998*

Script available from Playwrights Canada Press

•

Sophie ran away from her girlfriend, Baal, because she couldn't cope with
their relationship. She has since returned, very suddenly and unexpectedly.

•

Lights up on SOPHIE alone.

SOPHIE   I was in this guy's car. We were in the back seat—and he had the
radio on. You know—it was a way of making things feel more relaxed
and normal or something—like we were a regular boyfriend and girlfriend or something. So he had the radio on, and it was good, it was
helpful—I was... half-listening to it, you know? And suddenly
it was Baal singing right? It was the first time I ever heard her on the
radio. And I heard her voice—and it was like—my *real* lover's voice—
but it was *his* body. And it fucked me up—because I didn't wanna start
blending those two together.

So I quit. I kinda froze actually. And he got upset—and I told him
I suddenly felt sick, and I say, "Sorry, sorry"—you know—and I gave
him his money back. He was okay about it—he wasn't a bad guy—
he just kinda finished up without me, and then he drove me back to
where he picked me up. And then I got this panicky feeling—a feeling
that I had to *move* on. I suddenly felt like I had to find Baal. So I made
some calls, grabbed some stuff, jumped on a bus and I found her.

SOPHIE pauses and licks her lips.

...My mouth's dry...

I felt like Baal was my first lover. I feel like I was a virgin before I met Baal. And I mean—I wasn't. My older sister used to set me up with guys from the time I was ten years old. She got her boyfriends to train me—I don't know why. But I don't blame her either. I knew she just needed me to get involved, somehow. And it seemed normal to me. I though that was what you did.

Like my sister and I would go to this pizza joint, and this guy would be playing guitar and singing or something and she'd say, "Do you want him?" And I didn't even get what she meant, right? "Do you want him?" she says. And I'm like…

   SOPHIE shrugs.

…Okay…

But when Baal touched me—something shifted inside me. It was like—for the first time I *wanted* to be touched. Even when I got close to her—when I just stood beside her—I felt like I was coming already. And guys never did that for me; I did that for them. And I even thought maybe I couldn't come like that. I thought maybe I live in my head too much. I mean—I touch myself, I do—but I've always got these really degrading fantasies in my head, right? And I come and it's like this mixture of arousal and rage. So I thought maybe I could never really be with someone in a tender way—like really be *present*—and come. But then when Baal put her hands on me and touched me I came *so easily.* And I cried too. I cried and I cried. And it felt good to cry. I was proud to find a desire living in me that's so stubborn and so vulnerable.

When I left Baal I just wanted to be different. I needed to be tougher. I had to go out and take a lot of lovers and rip open those places she'd traced with her fingers—because I couldn't stand knowing that it didn't mean as much for her as it did for me. She wanted to make love where she pleased—and I couldn't make sense out of the way that meant other people.

Sometimes you meet somebody—and you know that you're gonna have to learn something really hard with them. And in that moment— you can either turn away—or you can decide that this is something you really need to know.

Beaver

by Claudia Dey

Premiered at Factory Theatre, Toronto, 2000

Script available from Playwrights Canada Press

•

The day after Rose Jersey's funeral—mother to Beatrice Jersey, 12.
That morning, Beatrice is moved out of her mother and father's home
and into her aunt Nora's. This is where we find her later that night.

•

BEATRICE takes a deep breath. NORA fills the kettle.

BEATRICE   I walked along the highway after I left here. Where are ya
boys? Where are ya? Don't ya see my thumb? Wha', is it still too small
for a ride? Don't ya see my legs? Still too small for a ride? Don't ya see
me? Heh? Come on boys. Don't ya see me? Hey, here. I'm here. Still too
small for a ride. So I run out in front o' the headlights. Honk, honk,
blow me over with your eighteen-wheeler. Not an eighteen-wheeler,
but a ZR-1. Wow. *(She laughs.)* A ZR-1. It's so shiny, so white, my eyes
water.

I open the door.

We hear "Remember" (Walking in the Sand) by Aerosmith.

I slam it behin' me an' slide over beside 'im, the gear shif' between my
legs. We drive along the highway. Music's on loud. Windows're down.
He drives faster 'n a train. My hair flies back. My eyes water. He bangs
the steerin' wheel 'n grins at me. Sorta gross but I don' care. He sings
an' the truck starts to smell like booze an' smokes an' burgers.

(singing) Oh no, oh no, oh no no no,
remember walkin' in the sand,

remember walkin' hand in hand,
remember the night was so exciting,
remember her smile was so enlightenin',
remember then she touched my cheek,
remember with her fingertips,
softly, softly we made it with a kiss.

He turns down the stereo. "My team calls me Toaster. You?" Beatrice. He pulls over on the shoulder. By Sauvé's Lumberyard.

We hear "Beast of Burden" by the Rolling Stones.

"Sauce? Sauce an' a smoke?" Sure, I say. He pulls out a six-pack an' gives me a beer. I tip it back an' drink it in one gulp.

"Thirsty." He grins. Never been so thirsty, Toaster, I say. He gives me another. I tip it back. He grins. Never been so thirsty, Toaster. He gives me another. I tip it back. Never been so thirsty, Toaster. Never been so thirsty. Never been... *(She burps.)* Ya wanna go to Toronto?

"Can't. Got practice in the mornin'." Oh. It's okay. You wanna, you wanna?... My mother's dead, Toaster, it's okay. It's okay.

I put his hands on my bare legs which are cold as cutlery an' I move 'em up an' up. He pushes my hips over, into the backseat. My boots hit the window. He clears the hockey sticks 'n I pull 'im down on me, my beast, I pull 'im down. Peel me away like the skin of a fish. Here's my backbone. Be careful.

'N he says. "You're so... I love your fuckin'. I love your.... You're so..."

Come on Toaster, come on. Come on, Toaster come on. Come on, Toaster come one. Come on. I'm punchin' 'im 'n tuggin' at his jacket. I'm pullin' 'is hair. I'm bitin' 'is wrist. Come on, Toaster. Come on.

She takes a deep breath.

"Beatrice Beatrice Beatrice Beatrice Beatrice Beatrice Beatrice Beatrice Beatrice Beatrice Beatrice Beatrice Beatrice Beatrice Beatrice Beatrice."

She takes a deep breath.

I fin' the door handle an' push it open. I fall out o' the truck, onto the gravel, onto my knees. My legs're wet 'n the world is so quiet my ears are bleedin'. From a mile away, I hear him say: "Sorry for takin' you so young Beatrice. Sorry for takin' you so young."

Oh, I'm not so young no more Toaster.

The Shape of a Girl

by Joan MacLeod

*Premiered at Alberta Theatre Projects, Calgary,
co-produced with Green Thumb Theatre, 2001*

Script available from Talonbooks

•

Braidie is referring to newspaper stories she has been reading
about the murder of a fourteen-year-old girl whose
attackers were, primarily, a group of girls.

•

BRAIDIE   The girls who beat her up, the girls who are on trial for
assault, they used to hang out at Wal-Mart. They also hang out *under
cover*. This sounds way cooler than it is. Because under cover really is
just that—a covered area at the school just like we had for playing
hopscotch when it rained. Granted these are tough girls. They make
like they are a gang and that they're all hooked up with the gangs in
New York and L.A.

On Granville Mall once Adrienne and me were followed by some
tough girls, these wipe out girls. They wanted us to give them some
money and Adrienne said no way. They said they were going to get us.
One gobbed on the back of Adrienne's jeans. But we weren't afraid of
them. We just thought they were idiots.

These girls in Victoria, they're a mess. Some are in foster care, some
have been doing the McFamily thing for a long long time. Some have
already been up on charges, one for lighting fire to another girl's hair.
The fight with the dead girl starts when someone butts out a cigarette
on her forehead. This is terrible enough in itself but it also opens
a door. *Look what I did? Now just watch, just wait and see….* It's surreal.
And that's not fair to say because it's exactly the opposite—it's totally
real. I mean it happened. And what scares me, what freaks me right

out, Trevor, is that I know the way in. I don't know how else to put it. I know the way in.

The human body is what? Eighty percent water? That kills me. We're like these melons with arms and legs. Well eighty percent of the female brain is pure crap. We're constantly checking each other out, deciding who goes where, who's at the bottom.

When I look at her picture, when I look at the picture of the dead girl in the paper, part of me gets it. And I hate it that I do, I hate to be even partly composed of that sort of information. But right now, if you put me in a room filled with girls, girls my age that I've never seen before in my life—I could divide them all up. I could decide who goes where and just where I fit in without anyone even opening their mouth. They could be from this island, they could be from Taiwan. It doesn't matter. Nobody would have to say a word. You know something, Trevor? I could have divided up a room like that when I was in grade two. Grade fucking two.

The Red Priest (Eight Ways to Say Goodbye)
by Mieko Ouchi

Premiered at Alberta Theatre Projects, Calgary, 2003

Script available from Playwrights Canada Press

·

"Woman—A Dream"

This piece was originally performed with the second movement
(Largo) of Summer from "The Four Seasons" by Antonio Vivaldi.
The play is set in May 1740. The Woman is a young French aristocrat
who has been married off to a powerful and cruel, and much
older courtier and patron of the arts in the court of
King Louis XV in France. Theirs is a loveless marriage.

·

WOMAN   A dream.

I'm standing in my room. It's my wedding day. I'm standing in
my corset and paniers. My arms out, I turn slowly as three young
serving girls blow the finest white powder onto my body off pieces of
parchment. Three young girls, no older than me. They blow and blow
until I am covered from head to toe with the finest mist of powder.
A ghost. They slowly turn me to face the mirror. They lift the heavy
gown over my head and dress me without disturbing a particle. They
place the lace veil on my head. It's time. They lead me outside. To
the church. To the waiting crowds inside. To my Mother and Father.
Father: austere and nodding. Pleased. Mother: unclear. A mixture of
hope and fear together. They all look at me expectantly. I walk down
the aisle. See him there. Every muscle in my body is telling me to run
and yet I continue towards him. One foot after the other. My blood
is in my ears. Pounding with every heartbeat. I can't breathe. I reach
his side. We turn to look at each other. He's old. With stern eyes and
a tight mouth. I feel my breath leaving me.

Then suddenly, somewhere, I hear the tiny bell-like sound of the tap of a baton on the edge of a music stand. And then like from heaven, a sound.

A choir of girls.

I look up but I can't see them. They're hidden behind the grills, but I can see their eyes and their mouths as they begin to sing, through the diamond shaped holes of the screens. The Cardinal is speaking. The singing gets louder and louder. Now my husband. His voice drowned out by the voices of the girls as the piece builds. He looks expectantly at me now. Sharp eyes focused on my lips. Waiting for me to speak, but the girls are like thunder now. And in an instant, I am one of them. My breath is their breath. Their eyes are my eyes. My voice is their voice.

And with the last echo of their voices as they finish, I'm gone.

Born Ready

by Joseph Jomo Pierre

Premiered at Theatre Passe Muraille, Toronto,
co-produced with Obsidian Theatre Company, 2005

Script available from Playwrights Canada Press

•

"Peggy Sue"

Peggy Sue, a 9mm Ruger, describes the fatal confrontation between
Blackman and B-side. Both are men whose lives mirror each other.
Both are men she has loved, Black Man kills B-side.

•

PEGGY SUE   It started with two guns.
One black and one chrome.
A Glock and a Ruger.
2 clips checked twice to make sure that they full.
Safetys' off, gotta make sure them safetys' off.
Placed in the waists of sizes 38, 34.
Probably a couple sizes too big for the frame they on.
There's a motherfucker here,
And over there something about somebody's mother cunt.
There's a fuck you, and a fuck you,
What you gonna do, and what you gonna do,
Yeh nigga, what nigga.
And they chest start heaving,
And the blood start pumping,
And they eyes get red,
Cause the anger's breathing.
Somebody gets pushed,
Somebody pushes back.
Somebody gets bitch slapped,

Now you know a nigga ain't having that.
So the fingers become fists,
And the bones be bricks.
Blowweeee!!
There's a tremor in his body,
As his flesh vibrates.
Powww!!
There's an elbow in the rib,
As the spine rotates.
Poww!! Pow! Poww!!
Combination of blows,
Roy Jones in they veins.
But he ain't backin down,
And he ain't backin down,
So a leg is raised
And a foot connects,
So a leg is raised again,
But this time it's snatched,
And a nigga falls back,
Right flat on his back.
But that pavement ain't so soft,
It ain't so forgiving.
You know that shit ain't so soft,
That shit ain't so forgiving.
So he grits his teeth,
And he curls his lips,
His nostrils flare
Those broad black nostrils flare,
And he's sucking, sucking, sucking,
Gasping for air.
Cause who's this mother fucker really think he is,
That I'll be bitched in these streets like this.
Disrespected in my own fuckin streets like this!
That's what he's thinking.
So I'm drawn,
Shit I'm looking pretty in the light.
The sudden power,
Revitalizes his body,
And he springs to his feet.

You ain't so fucking bad now huh?
All that tuff shit, where all that tuff fucking shit at now huh?
"Fuck you nigga, fuck you!"
Fuck me? Fuck me? Nahh fuck you!
And as they fucks collide,
He sees something in that other niggas eye.
Something resonates,
But he can't finger it.
There's something in that niggas eye.
There's a flash of a hand,
To the pocket with the Glock.
So I'm forced,
To the temple of a dome.
There's something in that niggas eye.
He really doesn't know what started this shit,
Or what it was that escalated this shit.
Why the two-tone chrome had to leave his hip.
Something.
He's caught in the middle of a thought,
By a hand that's too impatient to wait.
The same hand that reached for the Glock,
Once again tests it's faith.
Placca!!!
I deliver his faith.
It's called learnt reaction,
Or muscle memory.
Placca!!!
He said he saw himself in his eyes,
He said he heard himself in his voice,
And if he coulda stopped time,
Or put his fingers on pause,
He woulda asked him,
What's his name? Where's he from?
But there's no stopping this time.
There's no pause in this life.
And though that nigga's every movement was his,
Instinctual reactions that only living his life coulda bring,
He said he musta been crazy,
He said it just couldn't be.

That nigga had a different mother,
That nigga had a different father,
That nigga was a couple of shades different,
That nigga couldn'ta been me.
He's convincing himself,
That nigga couldn'ta been me.
But I know that niggas eyes.
I've felt that niggas touch.
I've seen that niggas soul.
Yeh, yeh, yeh,
Different mother, different father, different shade.
But,
He was you.
Suicide it's a suicide.

The Adventures of a Black Girl in Search of God
by Djanet Sears

Premiered at the duMaurier Theatre Centre, Toronto,
co-produced by Obsidian Theatre Company and Nightwood Theatre, 2002

Script available from Playwrights Canada Press

•

A capella voices moan, the lights up at the front of the stage.
The Chorus moves and dances into existence the water
that makes up the living creek. Rainey enters from the porch
and makes her way down to the edge of the creek.

•

RAINEY   "What do you eat?"

She looks out at the audience.

What do you eat. Asking me like she's my God damn mother or
something—I hate it when they do that. See, she doesn't know what
I know she's some second rate, just finished her residency, walk-in
clinic, witch-cum-doctor.

"Why, whadda you eat?" That's what I was gonna tell her right to her
big ass face. But then she wouldn't write me a prescription and that's
why I'd stopped there in the first place seeing as how I couldn't drive
anymore—retching cinders and cotton balls onto my lap and all over
the God damn steering wheel. And I'm supposed to meet Michael—
and I can do Toronto to Negro Creek in just over an hour if no one's
looking—but there I am on Avenue Road and Bloor getting the third
degree just to get some meds, and trying to figure out how I'm going
to stay over at Pa's when I can't use his toilet. He used to wash toilets,
was a sleeping car porter on Canadian Pacific, for years before anyone
would hire him as a lawyer. Says he could wash a toilet bowl so clean
you could lick the rim, the thought of which really makes me feel like

retching all over again, 'cause I can't hardly look at a toilet bowl anymore, even if it's on TV—'cause of Janie. I can't use any other toilet but my own.

She begins to form small mounds of dirt. She takes a Ziploc bag out of her pocket and carefully places the earth in the bag. She is methodical.

"I haven't been eating too well. Chronic lesser curve peptic gastritis," falls quickly out of my mouth. Medicalese for stomach ulcers. 'Cause I've been to med school too and I know, I want her to know that. And I know she hears it 'cause while she's looking down her nose at me, her big ass eyes nearly fall out of her big ass head.

RAINEY takes a morsel of earth and places it delicately on her tongue, savouring it.

I should have told her to prescribe Omeprazole or a prostaglandin. Better yet 2g of Sucralfate a half-hour before I eat. Instead I say, "I don't eat well."

I don't eat well, I know that. What am I gonna tell her, for Christ's sake? I'm an obstetrician? Haven't practiced in three years? That it started when Janie was still inside me. Me, secretly binging on freezer frost from the old fridge we'd bought in Fergus before Martha, my mother who raised me, before Martha passed—I hate that word— "passed." Gone on. Like there's something to go on to.

I could tell her the truth, tell her I've been trying to get out of here all my life and now, now I just hunger for the soft sugary earth by Negro creek. My Pa's family's lived and died on this bush land—been ours since the war of 1812. Maybe that's why it tastes so sweet. My great grandmother gave her life to this water trying to save a soldier's uniform. Lorraine Johnson. I was named for her.

Her grandfather Juma, Juma Moore was granted this Ojibway territory for fighting against the Americans in the Coloured Militia. Once a year his uniform would get a ritual cleaning.

A soldier's jacket appears and floats above the bodies that make up the water.

They'd go in the water with it, hold it under, and let the creek purify it. Lorraine had done it for years, but this time…. Well, she was in the water when it happened. The uniform slipped down, out of her hands and she went after it.

The jacket begins to float along the creek and a woman rises out of the water in pursuit of it. Both the jacket and the woman are enveloped by the flood of bodies.

They found her downstream when the creek thawed that spring, her hands still gripping that jacket. The authorities returned the body but kept the uniform—said it was the property of Her Majesty's army. They can be like that sometimes up here in God's country. Christ, they can be like that in the city.

I should have told her, I should have just told her, told her now since Janie, I yearn for chalk to dry the flood inside me and that's why I pop aspirins, only 35 on good days, not just any, it's got to be Bayer, original, not extra strength or that Life Brand shit, just Bayer acetylsalicylic acid, and that's why I've got me a hole in my belly— it's white willow bark. Aspirin, it's willow bark. So I've got a tree growing inside me. And I can't take the iron pills I need. Any doctor worth her salt knows that the intentional and compulsive consumption of non-food substances is eradicated with a forceful regimen of iron. But I can't hold something that heavy inside me—falls through the holes in my belly when I swallow and when it stays down, it bungs me up so bad I have to sit on a toilet for days, and I don't like to sit down on toilets, since Janie. Could you just see her face if I told her I was now eating ashes from cigarettes, not that I smoke them or anything, it's just, well, I don't know why, and it's got to be Export A, and I don't know why Export A. I'm just praying…. Funny, I'm praying a lot lately. I don't know why I do that either. I don't even know that I'm praying. Praying for one more aspirin before my guts fold into my spine, or I'm praying to reach the toilet, in my house, before I weep all over the floor. I'm not praying to God though. God, the Father. No father of mine would allow Janie…

RAINEY searches out a new section of earth and begins to discard the top layer of dirt with her hands.

I can still feel her…. Wrapped around me. She would hug me round my waist so tight sometimes like she was trying to get back inside me, like I was her fingers and toes and she'd missed having them around her all day, like I was her everything. She was…

Janie on the toilet—that's all I remember sometimes—that's my only image of her. Janie on the toilet holding my hands. Five and frail with a fever and I can fix her, there's a doctor in the house, Pa's house. And it's late. We'd been running through the woods all afternoon, she loved the woods so much, laughing and yelling for me, and she's got a fever and her neck hurts, but we've been running. And I send Pa with my car to get some Tylenol, Children's Tylenol, and she's on the toilet, so clean she could lick the rim and I'm holding her, holding her on the toilet and, and she, she, she, she…. She falls, falls… on me. And I can't find the keys to Pa's car and I'm running…. Running her through the middle of Holland Township, wishing I had wings, feeling her slip away from me, going somewhere without me—she always, always, always wanted me to come along with her before.

She's gone. They tell you she's gone. She's in my arms, I'm looking at her and and where's she gone. She's in my arms. I see her little copper feet, I see her tiny brazened fingers, her gilded neck, her coral lips… I know I'm looking at her. And I know… I know she's not there. And I'm, I'm, I'm… I'm wondering where she went. And you feel… I feel…

RAINEY looks up at the sky, trying to dam a stream of tears flooding up inside her.

Ten billion trillion stars in the universe. Ten billion trillion stars. That's not even counting the planets revolving around them. But it's mostly dark matter. It's 99% empty. One huge vast realm of nothingness.

I, Claudia

by **Kristen Thomson**

Premiered at Tarragon Theatre, Toronto, 2001

Script available from Playwrights Canada Press

•

Claudia, a prepubescent girl, in the boiler room
of her elementary school, addresses the audience.

•

CLAUDIA   Ever stare at yourself so hard that your eyes practically start
bleeding? I do.

I invited some girls over to my house to work on our science fair topic.
Ya, well, most of them didn't want to come. I don't know. I don't live in
the same neighbourhood as them anymore so they said it was too far
on the subway to get to my house. But I don't think that's true 'cause
it only takes me twenty minutes to get home. So I think they might be
lying. I don't know maybe their parents are stunned and don't let them
go on the subway at night, so maybe that's possible. Some parents are
very over-protective of their children. And then others, then some
others educate their children to be street smart. And I'm street smart.
Yeah. I went to a workshop one weekend with my mother. Well she
thought it would be a good idea because now I have to take the subway
from my house *and* from my house at my dad's. Some people would
say that downtown Toronto is not very safe. But I would not say that at
all, right. I would not say that at all. What I think is if you are someplace where there's nobody there then that's not safe because there's
nobody else to kind of protect you or to see, or to see if you might be
in trouble. So that's what I say is not safe. If nobody is there to watch
you. Right? So, safety is a very big concern for me. Yeah. Yes, it's a very
big concern for me for very sickening reasons because you know there
are vulnerable people in this society, and I am one of them. Like if

I lived on a farm, if I was like a farm girl, then maybe it wouldn't be so scary just to be alive. Except I might be afraid of getting my hand severed off by a machine. But I live in a very major urban centre and women and children... which is not to say that, not to say, I mean, I know that there are also racist crimes and there are kinds of crimes against people because of their sexuality and there are also crimes against people like if they are poor. Terrible things happen to poor people. I already know that. I already know that. And I know, I know that I am not poor. Like financially, I'm not very poor at all. Except I'm an only child so I am sibling poor. So, I don't have enough siblings. But I have goldfish. Romeo and Juliet. Two fish, they're really nice and they... I think Romeo might be pregnant. Yeah! Because I got them mixed up. I think that Romeo is a girl and Juliet is a boy! Yeah! I know! But it's hi-larious but it's true. Life is like that sometimes, isn't it? Life is sometimes... sometimes life is so true, it's hi-larious! Don't you find that? So anyway, I think they might be having children, like guppies. Um, is that what you call baby fish? Guppies? And I tell you, that's very satisfying for me. Yeah. And also I want a hamster for my room at Dad's. So cute. Well because in science class we're dissecting frogs, right, so, I don't want a frog because I've already seen one dead. But, but anyways I want a hamster and some gerbils. Something just like, I don't know, just to like enrich my life so I had like a wilderness in both my bedrooms. Like wildlife. Like a eco-system of two apartments and I would be like the migrating bird with two nests, but not like north and south. More like messy and clean. Yeah! My room at my mom's, which is my house, is the messy room. Well, it was the messy room. But my mom said I had to clean it 'cause it was a pigsty with my clothes for carpeting, plus, she said she was going to go through everything with a fine-tooth comb because—now I'm totally embarrassed.

Because I'm going through puberty. Oh my God, I don't even want to talk about it, it's disgusting! Yeah, like oh, oh "you're going through puberty" and everybody thinks they can say things like about if you need a bra or something. It's so embarrassing! It's so disgustingly embarrassing! And you can't even say anything, you can't even say, you can't even say, "STOP IT! STOP IT! STOP IT! STOP TEASING ME!" Right? 'Cause everybody thinks it's so funny and everybody all the grownups think because they went through it they can just torment you! But they can't. It's totally disgusting and unfair.

As she talks, CLAUDIA gets a snack from her lunch box. She takes out a single man's sock with something in it. She takes a juice box from the sock, sips as she continues to speak, and just tosses the box away carelessly whenever she's finished with it. CLAUDIA should drink as many juice boxes as she wishes throughout the show.

So anyways, because I'm growing, she said she wanted to take a bunch of my stuff that doesn't fit me anymore to the Goodwill and so she said—I had to go through all my stuff, get rid of everything I didn't want anymore and then she said she was gonna go through it all with a fine-tooth comb. My own *Private*! My own *Private* Sanctuary or Domain! She was gonna go through it with a *Fine-Tooth Comb*, that's what she said, you know, exact words, *Fine-Tooth Comb*!

Well, I had some very private objects in my room that isn't stuff I want to give away and isn't stuff that my mom is allowed to comb through. Like, there were things hidden underneath my bed. Like Evidence and secret objects, and personal musings. Like, essentially the whole stock of my private emotional life which I so can't let my mom see and I so can't put it at my dad's because a lot of it is stuff that I... well, um... I kind of... took... or—as the police would say, stole from his apartment. So I can't really put it there 'cause I only get to see him once a week, so he can't think that I'm, like, his criminal daughter who steals from him.

So I brought it all to the school, down here in the basement, in the boiler room, where nobody goes, except me. Weird and mysterious, eh? Oh, and except the janitor, but he doesn't even wreck it for me, he just leaves me alone. So now this is where I hide my stuff. Men's socks go in here.

She jams the sock back into an electric box which is already crammed with socks, and from various hiding spots she produces other objects.

DIARY. Sex book. This very terrible coffee mug. Baggy full of hair. Bunch of other stuff. And, on Tuesday mornings, which is the worst day of my entire life, I even come down here to hide my face.

Monologues

male

Walking on Water

by Dave Carley

Premiered at Prairie Theatre Exchange, Winnipeg, 2000

Script available from Signature Editions

•

The time is 1949 and the setting is the Munro Island on Lake Kawartha.
Lee Kwan is the chauffeur for the Munro family and he has taken
Mrs. Munro north to pick flowers. She begins prying into his personal life,
wondering if there might be a young woman back in town for whom he'd
like to take flowers. Lee was born in China and was sent to Canada to
join his father; shortly after his arrival the "Exclusion Act" was passed,
prohibiting Chinese women from immigrating to join their spouses.
So Lee has grown up in an all-male society of bachelor men, but he does
remember the kindness of the mother of a childhood chum, Max Bloom.
Max's mother is dying—and Lee would, in fact, like to take flowers to her.

•

LEE   *(over latter, to SADIE)* My only real friend. When I was a boy, he was
the only one who asked me to his house, ever. And Mrs. Bloom always
insisted I stay for dinner. My uncle—he was raising me after Dad
died—he'd allow it, but under protest. *(shrugs)* They were Jews; he
probably thought they'd try to circumcise me. Excuse me. One
summer—I was ten—Mrs. Bloom asked if I wanted to stay over. I said
no, I didn't. I did want to, but I knew Uncle would say no. That's not
true. I said no, because I wasn't sure how they slept. I knew it wasn't
four to a room like me and my uncle and two of the other Sunrise
waiters, three snorers and me. But you don't say no to Mrs. Bloom. She
went to the laundry and in front of everyone she told Uncle: "Lee's
staying over; get his toothbrush."

(addressing the audience by now) But, by eleven, she's having major
regrets; she's yelling at us to shut up and then she comes to the room.

Lights out. She goes over to Max and I see her shape in the dark, I see her lean over his bed for a moment—she's murmuring something I can't hear. Then she comes to my bed. I'm terrified. Terrified, curious too—what is this crazy woman doing, this "mother" doing. And she does this: she pulls the covers up around me, she leans over and says something, not English, for sure not Cantonese. I'm pretending to be asleep, I feel her breath, and then she kisses my forehead. First kiss.

As soon as she's gone, Max wants to talk again, but I don't. I need to think. And this is what I thought. "This is what it's like. This must be what a mother does. This must be what happens in a family." And I swore, with all the ferocity a ten-year-old can muster, someday I will get this for myself.

Burning Vision

by Marie Clements

Premiered at the Firehall Arts Centre, Vancouver, 2002

Script available from Talonbooks

•

Fat Man looks at the kid and hands him a bowl of Kraft Dinner.

•

FAT MAN   Who doesn't want to go back inside. Inside what is the question? All I got is this hole. We are all in a hole if that makes you feel better. All of us. You, me, everyone. The hole is getting bigger. Now, I didn't say because us people were getting bigger, us people, Americans. I said "The hole is getting bigger, deeper."

> *LITTLE BOY begins to play with the Kraft Dinner, taking the pieces and sticking them on the side of the chair.*

Like we are digging a hole so deep none of us will be able to get in, or out, because the hole is getting filled with all those immigrants: Asians, and Pakistanis and Hindus and Indians. I'm no racist, I'm just saying nobody knows their place. Nobody knows they've been conquered. They just keep it coming. Stretching the hole deeper with immigration, and retribution. Soon there's nothing left.

> *LITTLE BOY nods.*

You hear that? Pretty soon... nothing left. Shit, I should write a song and get a bunch of hippies on a mountain holding hands so they could sing.... "We are the world, we are the people.".... We are the fuckin' hole. We have made it big... and it's getting bigger, and bigger, talking to little Do Suzie Wong down the street, having to listen to Little Bear in the sticks, getting bigger, growing a big empty auditorium where we can all sit down together, and cry, fornicate our genes, and blow the fuckin' place out of the universe.

Orders

by Sandra Dempsey

Script available from Brooklyn Publishers

•

Rwanda, Africa 1994. Canadian Army Corporal First Class
Fred Crickland is twenty years old. He and his unit have been sent to
Rwanda under the auspices of the United Nations to try to bring
peace and order to the two warring ethnic groups: majority Hutus [1]
and minority Tutsis. [2] The corporal is dressed in standard
jungle green fatigues and a combat hat, [3] tactical vest, [4]
and carries a standard issue C7A1 assault rifle.

•

CRICKLAND   *(quickly taking up a defensive position on the perimeter)*
We got a report of fightin' an' pretty quick we come up on a Tutsi
village with a few actual survivors. Or maybe they're moderate Hutus?
Who too? You, too?

(He pauses to survey the horrible scene before him.) Gruesome. Hacked
to bits. Not cute little bits like some stupid Tweety an' Sylvester thing—
bits like chunks of bright pink flesh in brown wrappers—from human
beings. *(toneless sing-song) Tut, Tut, Tutsi, don't cry; Tut, Tut, Tutsi
don't...* [5]

*(He circles the surrounding area, checking for the enemy, speaking
urgently.)* Th' interpreter says the ones that're left won't survive their
wounds, an' one o' th' families are dyin' of AIDS an' haven't much time

---

[1] *Hutus* pronounced *HOO-TOO's*
[2] *Tutsis* pronounced *TOOT-see's*
[3] Combat hat, not *helmet*
[4] Tactical vest—not bulletproof/resistant
[5] Song tune: "Toot, Toot, Tootsie, Goodbye" (Brenda Lee)

left anyway. Captain says we're gonna help 'em—dress their wounds, give 'em the morphine. He says we're gonna make 'em feel better an' stay with 'em to protect 'em in case the butchers come back. 'Says if we can make their last breaths on this earth a little less hellish, that's what we're gonna do. That's exactly what we're gonna do.

(He falls to one knee, guarding for his unit behind him.) "Multi-National Force" my foot. There's only us Canadians here in Rwanda. That's it. No British. No U.S. No French. No Germans. They all *said* they'd be here, as part of the UN Force. But then they decided "*no*"—'guess when there's no oil, there's no riches here fer th' taking, when there's no *strategic* purpose, it just doesn't matter as much. An' I guess when it's this kind of humanity, it doesn't matter as much, either. This *colour* of humanity, at least.

Oh, everybody an' his uncle is there *like Jack the Bear* in places like th' Balkans—our boys are there, too, *and* in Croatia, an' even Haiti, too. An' heck, our boys have been deployed on more peacekeeping missions than any other country in the world. But *nobody, NO-BOD-EE, no-BODY* came to Rwanda—'just us Canadians. We're it—*we're* the UN's *Multi-National Force.* Just us.

(The unit is suddenly fired upon. He falls to his stomach to take cover, his weapon facing the threat.) We're takin' fire! 'Captain puts me to cover our left flank. *(He scans the bush ahead of him.)* I'm scannin' for the puke that's unloadin' on us. Come one, where are ya, ya dirty puke butcher! Show me your face! *(He's fired upon.)* Ha! I see your smoke! I got ya, now!

(He tries to compose himself, taking a drink from his water canteen, checking back toward the enemy.) Some poor sap in A Company got sent back just two weeks or so ago. He just couldn't stop wakin' up screamin'—every night, wakin' up th' whole stinkin' camp. Screechin' bloody fear up into th' sky for everyone t' hear.

(He looks back, checking for his fellow soldiers, then yells back to them.) It's a KID! *(The shooting gets closer and he ducks down. His anxiety builds, his breathing increases, he wipes sweat from his face and the palms of his hands. He nods "affirmative" to his superior.)* "Take him"—that's it. He's ordered me to take him out. "*Corporal, kill that frickin' shooter.*"

(He rolls back into his prone shooting position—assuring himself.) I hear him, alright. I hear him. That's *all* I hear—an' my heart beatin'—'so hard it's gonna fly right outa my chest. I'm the defence for my unit. My buddies are disarmed, busy wrappin' up hacked flesh. It's all on me— I've gotta protect them. *(Throughout the following, he executes the actions described.)* Magazine tight—ya, like when was it ever *not tight* out here…. Okay, aim for that little patch of ebony brown in amongst all th' green—that tiny, soft nine-year-old skull—with th' bone still growing… *(He closes and opens his eyes slowly, then re-focuses.)* Steady the cross-hairs. Fire.

(almost robotic, actions now done in slow motion) I feel the finger pull, feel th' ol' recoil into my shoulder, watch the bullet fly… *(confused)* Slow? *(nodding)* Slow, straight an' slow, through th' thick, stinkin' heat an' th' drippin' humidity an' th' sweet sick stench of death, straight into the kid's head. A kid with an assault weapon as light as a toy—like it was just *made* fer kids.

(He stops the actions and speaks gently.) Just a *pop* sound. 'Nothin' like those stupid movies—no flying backwards, no exploding brains, no blood an' guts sprayed everywhere. Just a pop. Th' round finds th' sweet-spot—his tiny head snaps back, just a little, hardly much at all, an' he just crumples to th' ground—all of three an' a half feet to th' ground.

(quietly) If I ever *do* finally make it outa this place alive, it'll be maybe 'cause today was th' day my heart *just* about stopped beatin' altogether.

We'll pull back now—'take whoever's still alive an' keep 'em under cover an' safe, for however long it takes 'em t' die. Then we'll give 'em as good a burying as we can, as decent as we can, an' then regroup back to patrol.

(He raises up on his knees, his rifle lowered and held casually at his side. His energy is completely drained.) 'Guess that's what rank is. Rank's a *beauty*, right? Beauty, when ya get t' *give* th' order t' kill a kid. But when you're *takin'* orders t' kill a kid, rank *stinks*.

   Blackout.

The Shooting Stage
by Michael Lewis MacLennan

Premiered at Firehall Theatre, Vancouver, 2001

Script available from Playwrights Canada Press

•

"Walk-In Closet"

The Shooting Stage explores how boys become men, and how the
fortunate survive violence through acts of the imagination.
Elliot *(17)* is practicing a speech on his favourite subject,
imagining himself before his classmates and tormentors.

•

ELLIOT   "Ladies and Gentleman, I give you, the world expert on the
come-back sensation of the animal kingdom, heeeeeerrrrre's Elliot!"
Thank you, thank you, thank you. Now I'm sure you're all wondering
why I'm standing here wrapped in a feather boa. Well, I'll tell you: it's
in honour of my favourite creature of the sky, who just so happens to
be the topic of my biology assignment. Yes, ladies and gentlemen, the
trumpeter swan. With a snow-white body and ebony beak, trumpeters
have a deep, penetrating honk that warns…

> *ELLIOT pulls his hands out of boa "wings" to reveal that he holds
> a pen and file cards.*

…cut "penetrating" are you crazy? They'll laugh me out of the
classroom. Heathens. Let's just say a loud honk. *(returning to the
speech)* …a *loud* honk that warns it will fight any encroacher.

But catch a swan and it goes limp in your hands. *(crosses out,
chuckling)* Limp. Oh I don't think *that'll* fly. *(revising speech)* Swans
know when to give up.

Trumpeters were killed for their feathers, used for quills, feather boas, powder puffs, and other fashionable items. *(revising)* Yes. Fashionable items, that's good.

(speech) But then. In 1933 they looked around and the partay was o-ver! They figured only thirty trumpeter swans were left. They'd practically cleared the place. So what they did was, they made the swan an endangered species and preserved precious mating—

(revising) Mating. Hm, no—precious *nesting* grounds. Don't give those maniacs an inch.

(speech) Now, there are over 8,000 trumpeters. Last summer a swan stayed *here*, alone. They don't know why, but nature is returning, healing herself. Nobody remembers a trumpeter swan ever coming back here before. This year the swan may come back, and I personally am on the lookout for her.

Because when she flies overhead I can see her. I can see...

The bird, bird of fearless solitude, killed for your feathers, your beauty sacrificed, fly back. Fly back to me. Your blood runs like mine. And your cry, your call to me is a secret, an old code, a memory.

Alphonse

by Wajdi Mouawad

translated by Shelley Tepperman

*Premiered at duMaurier Theatre Centre, Toronto,
produced by Theatre Direct, 2002*

*Script available from Playwrights Canada Press (English)
and Leméac Éditeur (French)*

•

"Alphonse's Family"

During the preceding "prologue", the actor removed his
business suit, revealing a neutral boyish outfit underneath.
Now the actor addresses the audience. The story begins.

•

I have a little brother.
His name's Alphonse.
He's a brave kid, Alphonse: his green eyes look right at you. When
he walks down the street, people don't notice him. He doesn't want
anyone to notice him. Anyway, he's just not the kind of kid people
notice.
Tonight Alphonse didn't come home from school. My mother's sitting
in the living room, her knitting beside her.
My father's smoking by the wide-open window staring into the night,
my sister's asleep (actually she's pretending)
and me, I'm sitting in the kitchen, worrying about Alphonse. Where
the hell can he be? The little weasel.

Something must have happened or he would have called! the mother
exclaimed from the living room. The father turned and spit in her face
to shut her up.

The father had already thrown in the towel. It's understandable, he was too upset.
After working like a dog my whole life, sweating away my youth, sweating away my good looks, my elegance, all for my family.
And what a family!
An ugly wife who knits non-stop, a daughter who still isn't married and who nobody wants,
and an ungrateful son who just stands there in front of me smirking superciliously.
And the last one, the youngest.
Alphonse,
the one I'd put all my hopes in,
now he's gone. No-one knows where.
What have I done with my life? Why didn't I listen to myself back then "You aren't made to have a family" and now look what's happened! Your youngest son's just disappeared! I don't blame him, I'd have done the same thing!

Actually, Alphonse was walking along a country road but we're not supposed to know that just yet.

I really love Alphonse. He listens to me when I speak, and when I need help he's always there. Where is he? Life has given me nothing: my daughter's crying into her pillow, my son, the eldest one, must be reading in the kitchen (that one doesn't give a damn about anything!) and my husband who used to be so handsome, a man now all alone in life, a man who used to be so strong, has to steady himself on the door frame so he doesn't fall. My Goodness! They say it's going to be cold tomorrow. And Alphonse didn't take his sweater with him! I mustn't forget to buy cheese for tomorrow.
We mustn't scold Alphonse. We'll have to try and understand why he left. That's it.

In her bed, the sister started to cry. She had said one or two prayers but what good was that? Alphonse won't be coming back. She was used to looking after him. When he was little she took him for walks, she bathed him, she gave him little presents. He was her baby brother. At night, when Alphonse would awaken, she'd wake up right away too, stirred by a feeling of protectiveness.
Alphonse, where are you going? I'd ask every time.

I'm going to get a glass of water.
Do you want me to get it for you?
No thanks, sis, I need to stretch my legs.
He always said exactly the same thing: it was to stretch his legs!
But I know it was really to sneak into the pantry and stuff his face with marshmallow cookies.

Actually, the real reason Alphonse would get up was very very different…

The Red Priest (Eight Ways to Say Goodbye)
by Mieko Ouchi

Premiered at Alberta Theatre Projects, Calgary, 2003

Script available from Playwrights Canada Press

•

"Vivaldi—A Dream"

Antonio Vivaldi, the great Italian violin virtuoso and composer
is a year from his death and penniless, in the house of a rich
French patron to write a concerto. He arrives, only to discover
that the patron has made a bet with King Louis XV that Vivaldi
cannot teach his young wife to play the violin in six weeks.
Through the lessons, Vivaldi comes to know the sad young woman.

•

VIVALDI   A dream.

She is dressed in a gown of gold. She is at Versailles. In the Royal
Quarters… the suites that no outsider has seen but architects Louis Le
Vau and Ange-Jacques Gabriel. I hide myself in the shadows and watch
as she steps carefully up the Queen's staircase that leads to the luscious
gilt and blossom pink suite of rooms. One wall is covered in tall,
ornate glass doors, draped in heavy embroidered silk. She walks
towards them and throws one set open.

Ah… the light! *The Parterre du Midi*…. The Garden. Adorned with
statues and fountains. She is staring at something… to the west, at the
end of the Royal Walk, sits the Fountain of Apollo. Gold… glorious…
bathed in the light of the end of day, the sun god rises in his chariot
from the water. A chariot so full of life, I can feel the tug of the horses
on their bits as it strains to escape into the sky. She begins to run.

I follow her quickly out onto the terrasse… and down the graceful
curve of the staircase to the grounds…. She's so far ahead. She has

already reached the fountain. A distant figure as she pulls herself onto the thin stone ledge circling the fountain and without a thought. She leaps... towards the water... towards what? Freedom. The water breaks like a slap. I can't seem to see her... I can only imagine her corset tight like a watery embrace pulling her down. I want to save her. I can't seem to move... I'm paralyzed.... Whwa! She breaks through the surface... a swirl of silk and hair and arms.... She fights to move towards the chariot... but... too late. Apollo leaves without her. She screams to him as the chariot lifts off but he, like me, can't seem to hear her cries. I can only watch helplessly like her... his golden cape fluttering behind him as he travels up to the beckoning twilight, disappearing in its darkening embrace.

When I look back down, somehow, she has managed to reach the stone base where the chariot once stood... and pull herself gasping onto it. But as she stands forlornly watching his final ascent... the gold drips off her heavy dress with the water and the dress stiffens where it hangs like ice and she's frozen. She has become a statue. She has replaced him. Amongst the gilded legions of Greek Gods and Goddesses, she alone stands out. A grey, lone statue of a woman.

Made of stone and looking to heaven.

Earshot

by Morris Panych

Premiered at Tarragon Theatre, Toronto, 2001

Script available from Talonbooks

•

Lights up on DOYLE, sitting in a chair, his ear pressed to the wall.

DOYLE   Slowly. No; slowly. Let it just—no. *Slip diaphanously.* Honest to Christ. You let that wool skirt of yours drop like a dirty laundry bag, Valerie. Can't you just tease me a little? The bathwater's too hot, anyways. What's your rush, for God's sake? There will always be men, waiting in bars, anxious to pay you no attention. It's what men do. No; don't put anything on just yet. Let me admire the small of your back for just a little—ugh—I wish the stupid robe was at the very least silk. If I had the money—I don't like the way terrycloth grabs at your, at your—not that I blame it. At your skin. I'm just, just jealous, that's all. I'm jealous of your robe.

You see how you make me say the stupidest things?

As he slips a hand down his pants. Suddenly.

Honest to goodness, Mrs. Noon! Shut—up.

Nothing turns a person off like senile dementia.

Terrycloth doesn't suit you. Only the highest quality of everything. It's what your skin deserves. I've never heard such lovely skin. Even against the obscene lacerations of polyester and—viscose.

Sawing below.

What's he doing, now? If I had any concentration at all, these people would have thrown it right out the window.

The pantyhose, yes. That's it, that's it. Your lovely derrière slipping out, like, like—oh God. Two—poached—half-peaches? No; I diminish it with commentary. The sound, the sound of your little bum. Is there anything in words to describe it? Don't peel off the legs so quickly. The nylon against your leg stubble is all I live for.

Did I say "live"? God. Wait, the water's still too hot, Valerie, Don't— there. What did I tell you? You always pour it too hot, because you underestimate the delicacy of your skin. Not me. I would never do that. I would wash your back with a sponge so soft it probably wouldn't even be a sponge. It would probably just be the word "sponge," whispered over your shoulders. Like the breeze on a lake.

Mrs. Noon. Is that you eating, or is someone slapping a thick coat of paint on the walls with a raw piece of liver?

The thing is, you see, the truth of it is, I could never touch you with anything but the softest softness of my voice. The flesh is too coarse. This body too abrasive; with its hair and its elbows and its—its—No. I don't think you'd find me very pleasant company at all. To start with, I'm—well, I'm human. And you deserve better. And of course, I have this hearing—thing. This problem. As you know. Not that I have a problem with hearing. It's a problem, as you know, of hearing too much; which is really much more of a problem, as you know, than not hearing at all. Not deafness; *deafening.*

It was a kind of deafness at first. As an infant, I had tinnitus so extreme that no other sound could penetrate.

Sighs. Hammering below.

One can only hope he's building his own coffin down there.

Beat.

The ear-ringing condition suited me fine. I had no interest in the outside world. But fed up with my circumspection, and no doubt annoyed by my blissful indifference, my mother dragged me off to some dingy office above a button shop one day, where I was ushered behind a beaded curtain, by this blind Uzbeki woman; her thin cold fingers gripping the back of my neck. Everything smelled of tar. They had to hold my head down. The pain was—what's worse than unimaginable? And for what, Valerie? To become a freak of nature?

To spend the rest of my days hearing a pin drop. Did I say "drop"?
I can hear it *dropping*.

Beat.

My mother wanted me cured. What good was a child who not only
wouldn't listen; couldn't listen? Who would she complain to about her
swollen feet? Or order about like a servant; send out for cigarettes and
petroleum jelly.

Whatever they poured into my ears, it worked; if their intention was to
turn my life into a nightmare. The ringing stopped; my ears were
opened.

But did I need to know there were termites inside the walls? When you
can hear the blood coursing through your veins, Valerie, you can hear
too much. There are things, believe me, that a ten-year-old just doesn't
need to be exposed to. I knew, for instance, that my mother had men
over, now and again. But I never knew, until then, what her fingernails
sounded like, digging into their bare, writhing backs. The world
opened up like a big, giant, blaring trumpet and blasted me with its
horrors. The clamour of people, everywhere, weeping, suffocating,
ordering their french fries. What do you listen to, Valerie, when you
can hear everything?

At the heating vent.

Remple's nightly confessions? They're still scraping that buddy of his
off the bottom of the shipping crate.

Beat.

Don't go out tonight, Valerie.

Head leaning on the wall.

Fronteras Americanas

by Guillermo Verdecchia

Premiered at Tarragon Theatre, Toronto, 1993

Script available from Talonbooks

•

"Dancing"

Wideload offers some inter-cultural analysis.

•

Facundo, aka Wideload, addresses the audience.

WIDELOAD   Espeaking of music I haf to say dat I love de way you guys dance. I think you Saxons are some of de most interesting dancers on de planet. I lof to go down to the Bamboo when my friend Ramiro is playing and just watch you guys dance because you are so free—like nothing gets in your way: not de beat, not de rhythm, nothing.

What I especially like to watch is like a Saxon guy dancing wif a Latin woman. Like she is out dere and she's smiling and doing a little cu-bop step and she's having a good time and de Saxon guy is like trying really hard to keep up, you know he's making a big effort to move his hips independently of his legs and rib cage and he's flapping his arms like a flamenco dancer. Generally speaking dis applies just to male Saxon— Saxon women seem to have learned a move or two...

Of course part of de problem is dat you guys wear very funny shoes for dancing—I mean like dose giant running shoes with built-in air compressors and padding and support for de ankles and nuclear laces—I mean you might as well try dancing wif snowshoes on. Your feet have to be free, so dat your knees are free so dat your hips are free—so dat you can move your culo wif impunity.

So dere dey are dancing away: de Saxon guy and de Latin woman or de Saxon woman and de Latin guy and de Saxon, you can see de Saxon thinking:

Wow, he/she can really dance, he/she can really move those hips, he/she keeps smiling, I think he/she likes me, I bet he/she would be great in bed...

No dis is important so I'm going to continue talking about it—even though it always gets real quiet whenever I start in on this stuff.

Now dere are two things at work here: the first is the fact that whenever a Latin and a Saxon have sex it is going to be a mind-expanding and culturally enriching experience *porque nosotros sabemos hacer cosas que ni se imaginaron en la* Kama Sutra, *porque nosotros tenemos unritmo, un calor un sabor un tumbao de timbales de conga de candomble de kilombo. Uno onda, un un dos tres, un dos. Saben...?*

Dat's de first factor at work and for dose of you who want a translation of dat come and see me after de show or ask one of de eSpanish speakers in de audience at intermission.

De second factor is the Exotica Factor. De Latin Lover Fantasy. And I'll let you in on a little secret: Latins are no sexier dan Saxons—well maybe just a little. De difference is dis: we like it. A lot. And we practice. A lot. Like we touch every chance we get.

Now I doan want you to get de impression I'm picking on you Saxons. Nothing could be further from my mind... I have de greatest respect for your culture... and you know, every culture has its own fertility dance, its own dance of sexual joy—you people hab de Morris Dance, and hey, you go to a Morris Dance Festival and it's de Latinos who look silly. You have de Morris Dance—very sexy dance—you know, a bunch of guys hopping around wif bells on and every once in a while swinging at each other. Now, I am not doing de dance justice and I am looking for a Morris Dance teacher so if you know of one please pass deir name along. You have de Morris Dance and we have de mambo, de rumba, de cumbia, de son, son-guajiro, son-changui, de charanga, de meringue, de guaguanco, de tango, de samba, salsa... shall I continue?

The Monument

by Colleen Wagner

*Premiered at the Canadian Stage Company, Toronto,
co-produced with Necessary Angel and the Manitoba Theatre Centre, 1995*

Script available from Playwrights Canada Press

•

Stetko, a young soldier convicted of war crimes, is strapped
to an electric chair. A single bulb above him provides the only light.
He appears small in the vast darkness.

•

STETKO   The one I liked the best was 17, maybe 18.
And pretty. With watery eyes.
Like a doe's.
She was like that.

I was her first.
I mean, she was a virgin.
A man can tell.
She said she wasn't, but the way she bled—and cried—
I knew.

I didn't mean to hurt her.
Every time she cried out I pulled back.
I wanted it to last.

> *Pause.*

I don't care for orgasm like some men.
They only think about coming. They rush through like they're
pumping iron just wanting to come.
Not me.
Once you come that's it.
It's over.

And there you are facing the same old things that were there before you started.

I don't care for the world much.

(laughs) 'Course it doesn't care much for me either.
So big deal, eh?
It don't care for me, I don't care for it...
Big deal.

The doctors—make me laugh—they're trying to figure me out.
Why I'm like this.
Nobody agrees.
Dr. Casanova—Yeah! Casanova! I think he's joking when he tells me his name. I laugh in his face.
He stares back.
He's got eyes like a chicken's.
Beady.
And small.
So I don't say nothing.
We have one-hundred and six sessions and I don't say anything. Not a word. We stare at each other for one hour, one-hundred and six times.
He thinks I'm a "passive aggressive."
I think he's fucking nuts.

They bring in another doctor.
A woman.
She comes with a bodyguard.
'Cause I'm dangerous.
That's what the bodyguard said.
"Dangerous."
I say to her, "wanna fuck?"
She says, "and then go to the forest?"
I know what she's doing—egging me on.
Trying to trick me.
Get me to talk.
I look at her and I think, this doctor has never done it except in a nice soft bed and she doesn't do it much, and she doesn't like it when she does do it.
She's got a tight puckered mouth.

I said to her "Is your ass like your mouth?"
She says, "No. One exhales, the other inhales. Don't yours?"
She's funny. So I talk to her.
Except,
I don't tell her where the bodies are.

I don't remember.

Book and Script Publishers

Brooklyn Publishers, LLC
1841 Cord St.
Odessa, TX, 79762 USA
Phone: 888-473-8521
Fax: 432-368-0340
www.brookpub.com
info@brookpub.com

Cape Breton Books
42002 Cabot Trail
Wreck Cove, NS, B0C 1H0
Phone: 902-539-5140
Fax: 902-539-9117
www.capebretonbooks.com
bretonbooks@ns.sympatico.ca

Coach House Books
401 Huron St. on bpNichol Lane
Toronto, ON, M5S 2G5
Phone: 1-800-367-6360
Fax: 416-977-1158
www.chbooks.com

Great North Artists Management
350 Dupont St.
Toronto, ON, M5R 1V9
Phone: 416-925-2051
Fax: 416-925-3904
renazimmerman@gnaminc.com

Leméac Éditeur
4609, rue D'Iberville, 3rd floor
Montreal, QC, H2H 2L9
Phone: 514-524-5558
Fax: 514-524-3145
lemeac@lemeac.com

McArthur & Company
322 King Street West, Suite 402
Toronto, ON, M5V 1J2
Phone: 416-408-4007
www.mcarthur-co.com
info@mcarthur-co.com

Playwrights Canada Press
215 Spadina Ave., Suite 230
Toronto, ON, M5T 2C7
Phone: 416-703-0013
Fax: 416-408-3402
www.playwrightscanada.com
orders@playwrightscanada.com

Playwrights Guild of Canada
54 Wolseley St., 2nd Floor
Toronto, ON, M5T 1A5
Phone: 416-703-0201
Fax: 416-703-0059
www.playwrightsguild.ca
orders@playwrightsguild.ca

Scirocco Drama, an imprint of J.
Gordon Shillingford Publishing Inc.
PO Box 86, RPO Corydon Ave.
Winnipeg, MB, R3M 3S3
Phone: 204-779-6967
Fax: 204-779-6970
www.jgshillingford.com
jgshill@allstream.net

Signature Editions
PO Box 206, RPO Corydon Ave.
Winnipeg, MB, R3M 3S7
Phone: 204-779-7803
Fax: 204-779-6970.
www.signature-editions.com
signature@allstream.net

Talonbooks
P.O. Box 2076
Vancouver, BC, V6B 3S3
Fax: 604-444-4119
www.talonbooks.com
info@talonbooks.com

Author Index

Title Index